T0363984

PUBLISHED BY BOOM BOOKS

www.boombooks.biz

ABOUT THIS SERIES

....But after that, I realised that I knew very little about these parents of mine. They had been born about the start of the Twentieth Century, and they died in 1970 and 1980. For their last 20 years, I was old enough to speak with a bit of sense.

I could have talked to them a lot about their lives. I could have found out about the times they lived in. But I did not. I know almost nothing about them really. Their courtship? Working in the pits? The Lock-out in the Depression? Losing their second child? Being dusted as a miner? The shootings at Rothbury? My uncles killed in the War? Love on the dole? There were hundreds, thousands of questions that I would now like to ask them. But, alas, I can't. It's too late.

Thus, prompted by my guilt, I resolved to write these books. They describe happenings that affected people, real people. The whole series is, to coin a modern phrase, designed to push your buttons, to make you remember and wonder at things forgotten.

The books might just let nostalgia see the light of day, so that oldies and youngies will talk about the past and re-discover a heritage otherwise forgotten. Hopefully, they will spark discussions between generations, and foster the asking and answering of questions that should not remain unanswered.

BORN IN 1971?
WHAT ELSE HAPPENED?

RON WILLIAMS

AUSTRALIAN SOCIAL HISTORY

BOOK 33 IN A SERIES OF 35

FROM 1939 to 1973

BOOM, BOOM BABY, BOOM

BORN IN 1971? WHAT ELSE HAPPENED?

Published by Boom Books. Wickham, NSW, Australia

Web: boombooks.biz
Email: jen@boombooks.biz

© Ron Williams 2013. This edition 2023

ISBN: 9780648771661

Cover images: National Archives of Australia.

A1200, L95545, Duke of Edinburgh Tour 1971;

A1200, L94115, Long haired goat and kid held by Aboriginal and missionary Papunya;

A1200, L92764, Federation Cup held by L Hunt, Margaret Court and Evonne Goolagon;

A1200, L93287, Pope Paul's visit to Australia, 1971.

TABLE OF CONTENTS

IMPORTANT PEOPLE AND RECORDS

Queen of England	Elizabeth II
Prime Minister of Australia	John Gorton
.... After March	William McMahon
Leader of the Opposition	Gough Whitlam
Governor General	Paul Hasluck
Pope	Paul VI
PM of England	Edward Heath
President of America	Richard Nixon

WINNER OF THE ASHES

1968	Drawn 1 - 1
1970 - 71	England 2 - 0
1972	Drawn 2 - 2

MELBOURNE CUP WINNERS

1970	Baghdad Note
1971	Silver Knight
1972	Piping Lane

ACADEMY AWARDS

Best Actor	George C Scott
Best Actress	Glenda Jackson
Best Movie	Patton

INTRODUCTION

This book is the 33rd in a series of 35 books that I have researched and written. It tells a story about a number of important or newsworthy Australia-centric events that happened in 1971. **The series** covers each of the years from 1939 to 1973, for a total of 35 books.

I developed my interest in writing these books a few years ago at a time when my children entered their teens. My own teens started in 1947, and I started trying to remember what had happened to me then. I thought of the big events first, like Saturday afternoon at the pictures, and cricket in the back yard, and the wonderful fun of going to Maitland on the train for school each day.

Then I recalled some of the not-so-good things. I was an altar boy, and that meant three or four Masses a week. I might have thought I loved God at that stage, but I really hated his Masses. And the schoolboy bullies, like Greg Favvell, and the hapless Freddie Ebans. Yet, to compensate for these, there was always the beautiful, black headed, blue-sailor-suited June Brown, who I was allowed to worship from afar..

I also thought about my parents. Most of the major events that I lived through came to mind readily. But after that, I realised that I really knew very little about these parents of mine. They had been born about the start of the Twentieth Century, and they died in 1970 and 1980. For their last 20 years, I was old enough to speak with a bit of sense. I could have talked to them a lot about their lives. I could have found out about the times they lived in. But I did not. I know almost nothing about them really. Their courtship?

Working in the pits? The Lock-out in the Depression? Losing their second child? Being dusted as a miner? The shootings at Rothbury? My uncles killed in the War? There were hundreds, thousands of questions that I would now like to ask them. But, alas, I can't. It's too late.

Thus, prompted by my guilt, I resolved to write these books. They describe happenings that affected people, real people. In 1971, there is some coverage of international affairs, but a lot more on social events within Australia. This book, and the whole series is, to coin a modern phrase, designed to push the reader's buttons, to make you remember and wonder at things forgotten. The books might just let nostalgia see the light of day, so that oldies and youngies will talk about the past and re-discover a heritage otherwise forgotten. Hopefully, they will spark discussions between generations, and foster the asking and the answering of questions that should not remain unanswered.

The sources of my material. I was born in 1934, so that I can remember well a great deal of what went on around me from 1939 onwards. But of course, the bulk of this book's material came from research. That meant that I spent many hours in front of a computer reading electronic versions of newspapers, magazines, Hansard, Ministers' Press releases and the like. My task was to sift out, day-by-day, those stories and events that would be of interest to the most readers. Then I supplemented these with materials from books, broadcasts, memoirs, biographies, government reports and statistics. And I talked to old-timers, one-on-one, and in organised groups, and to Baby Boomers about their recollections. People with stories to tell came out of the woodwork, and talked no end about the tragic, and funny, and commonplace events that have shaped their very different lives.

The presentation of each book. For each year covered, the end result is a collection of short Chapters on many of the topics that concerned ordinary people in that year. I think I have covered most of the major issues that people then were interested in. On the other hand, in some cases I have dwelt a little on minor frivolous matters, perhaps to the detriment of more sober considerations. Still, in the long run, this makes the book more readable, and hopefully it will convey adequately the spirit of the times.

Each of the books is mainly Sydney based, but I have been deliberately national in outlook, so that readers elsewhere will feel comfortable that I am talking about matters that affected them personally. After all, housing shortages and strikes and juvenile delinquency involved all Australians, and other issues, such as problems overseas, had no State component in them. Overall, I expect I can make you wonder, remember, rage and giggle equally, no matter where you hail from.

BACKGROUND STORIES FROM 1970

The war in Vietnam. Last year, the Vietnam War occupied more Press space than any other story. You will perhaps recall that this war was really a battle between the forces of Capitalism and Communism which were both in a world-wide confrontation to decide which of them would win the hearts and fortunes of the rest of the world.

For the previous half decade, these two combatants, represented by the USA and China respectively, had chosen Vietnam as their battle-field, and had, with increasing ferocity, ravaged that country as their troops had found ways to kill each other. And at the same time, they manged to kill and maim millions of Vietnamese, and lay waste to their nation.

Sentiment in Australia about the war was very much divided. **One group supported the war. It cheered on the Americans troops**, supported as they were by Australian Army Regulars and young conscripts. It argued that **the Reds**, both Chinese and Russians, **were out to conquer the world**, and were intent on moving from a conquered Vietnam, down though Malaya and Singapore, until they raised their flag over their ultimate goal of Tasmania.

The other group was opposed to the war. They argued that the war was more a war of independence, and that it had started as a movement to remove the French colonisers from Vietnam. They thought that the US was there only for its own interests, and that they expected an easy victory. **Surely then the world would recognise that the US was the nation to ally with.**

But **many of these opponents** saw Vietnam as a place where their family members would be killed. Simple as that. Not much of the ideological argument here. **Just a fervent wish to have the Dads and Sons alive.**

For those who opposed the war, the Letter below gives some idea of their state of mind.

Letter, Helen Applebee. How-oh-how did we get into this war? And why-oh-why are we still in it? Our young lads, including my son, are fighting America's war in a land that we know nothing about, and which we will never know anything about. We are fighting on their soil, killing their people, and watching our own boys being killed every day.

We in Australia are not interested in the big bad Reds coming right across the Pacific to destroy our way of life. If they come near us, **then** we will fight them. What good does it do us if some stupid hill is fought over for ten days, and then won or lost? Or inevitably abandoned by both sides.

And what good does it do we citizens at home? Our taxes are increased, our supplies are reduced, our streets are filled with Yanks on leave. They eat the best food, wear the best wool, and seduce our best girls with promises of marriage and a life of bliss back home with Mom.

Where are our politicians? Cravenly following America's lead. If General MacArthur says jump, they all jump. We need our own foreign policy that serves our own interests and not those of some foreign bully like America.

Bring our boys and our men back home, and leave the war-mongers to do what they relish and do best - make war anywhere but home.

But **the supporters of the war** took a different tack. Here is one example of their arguments.

Letters, Lois Frame. Since WWII, the Russian Communists have captured all of eastern Europe and put it behind the Iron Curtain. They spent a fortune on bribing leaders in every nation in Africa, and now is moving to South America. It had frustrated all attempts as disarmament, and continued to build up its armed forces and weaponry. China has gone along with all this, and is now setting itself to invade south east Asia and Australia.

Importantly, the Communist system will destroy the initiative that can be found under capitalism. Look at the marvels that America has created around the world as its influence grows. And contrast that with the misery and servitude that Communism always brings.

We should keep in mind how quickly the South Pacific fell to the Japanese. If Vietnam falls, you could expect that the Reds would soon conquer poor defenceless Australia.

Do not be fooled. The defence of Vietnam is crucial for the defence of Australia.

We need this war. Our safety demands it.

By the end of 1970, everyone had forgotten the flimsy excuses for the war, and were sick and tired of it. Its futility was obvious and, from the American point of view, the bad behaviour of some American soldiers had turned much of its population against it.

In Australia, the two groups were publicly vocal, demonstrations in the street were everywhere every second day, vocal arguments sometimes violent, were common. Spoken contempt for another's views permeated society.

But the American distaste for the war was spreading into Australia as well. I suppose at the moment, about 60 per cent of our citizens thought that we should withdraw our troops from Vietnam.

Mothers, and families, of the lads conscripted were to the forefront in protesting that the boys should come home. They had seen their sons chosen by a lottery system **and** sent off to fight, and perhaps die, in a land that no one had heard of. And for what purpose? They argued there was no purpose.

So, at the start on 1971, the bitter arguments were set to continue, and the passions that had been stirred over the last few years were still there waiting for fresh ammunition.

Smoking is not a health hazard. The entire world, in its innocence, blithely lit up and smoked without any worries about health. Images of pretty men and women filled the media and screens, people talked about the benefits of smoking menthol flavoured cigarettes, and small lads and girls went to the corner store and bought fags without their mothers knowing.

There were a few studies starting to emerge that showed the link between smoking and cancer. But these were hush-hushed and scarcely saw the light of day. For the vast majority, smoking was glamorous. Any hint to the contrary was met with "Old Bill smoked for seventy years and he is still going."

Who could possibly argue against that?

Jack Mundy. Mundy was elected as Secretary of the Builders Labourers Federation (BLF) of NSW in 1968. From his position in this powerful Trade Union, he was in 1971 beginning to organise strikes against any new building activity that **did not conform to his Green standards**.

This meant that a decade of strikes and Green bans was ahead. This in turn resulted in many ugly confrontations on building lots and in the streets generally. For the Seventies, Mundy was a controversial figure and, for a time, his policies destroyed many large building projects in NSW and other States.

Cricket in politics. The idea, that the splendid game of cricket was just a game, took a big hit in 1970. In South Africa, the blacks were being dropped from national teams simply because they were black. To do this was consistent with the national policy of the Government there that had introduced a policy of Apartheid. That was to separate the blacks from the whites, and briefly, to give most opportunities to the whites.

In cricket, a number of international tours were on the agenda, and it was decreed that blacks would be excluded. This got a lot of people very excited and the opposition to the Apartheid policy grew apace. Australia, as the world's leading cricketing nation, was right in the thick of things.

Aborigines in Australia. In the 1960's, the attitude of the general public to Aboriginies had become more sympathetic than in earlier years. The Federal and State Governments had all enacted legislation and regulations that gave Aborigines a fairer go. This was accepted and mostly welcomed by the whites and some of the grosser injustices were removed. And it was generally recognised that there was still much to be done.

The problem was that no one had a clue about what the fix was. Not even the Aborigines. Over the next 50-plus years, well-meaning Governments and a host of other people, have made efforts to improve their lot, and some of these have had some success.

At the start of the Twenties, Aborigines are still a long way behind their white counterparts in their day-to-day living. No one person, group, or policy is apparent that will promote the equality that we all, **black and white**, would cherish.

Status of women. The widespread use of the Contraceptive Pill from the mid-sixties changed the game for many women. For example, they could now decide whether to have a child and when to have it, rather than gamble using other methods of control. But the Pill had disadvantages. For example, many Catholic women were left in a quandary. They wanted to enjoy its benefits, but were denied by edicts from their Church.

Hijacking. One activity that was gaining in popularity was the hijacking of planes. Para-military groups were prominent in doing this, but the range was wide. Sometimes **individuals** would have a go. For example, many a flight in America was diverted to New York in particular.

Authorities around the world were objecting to this. Part of the solution was to place armed guards on multiple planes, with the prospect of having gun battles at 30,000 feet. A more hopeful deterrent was to have a universal accord that said that wherever the plane landed, the villains would be captured and punished. This protocol was now close to acceptance around the world.

MY RULES IN WRITING

I give you a few Rules that I follow as I write. They will help you understand where I am coming from.

Rule 1. Throughout this book, I rely a lot on reproducing Letters from the newspapers. Whenever I do this, I put the text in a different font, and indent it a little, and make the font somewhat smaller. I do not edit the text at all. The same is true for the News Items at the start of each Chapter. **That is, I do not correct spelling or if the text gets garbled, I do not correct it. It's just as it was seen in the Papers.**

Rule 2. The material for this book, when it comes from newspapers, is reported as it was seen at the time. If the benefit of hindsight over the years changes things, then I might record that in my Comments. **The info reported thus reflects matters as they were seen in 1971.**

Rule 3. Let me also apologise in advance to anyone I might offend. In a work such as this, it is certain some people will think I got some things wrong. I am sure that I did, but please remember, all of this is only my opinion. And really, my opinion does not matter one little bit in the scheme of things. I hope you will say "silly old bugger", and shrug your shoulders, and read on.

So now we are ready to plunge into 1971. Let's go.

JANUARY NEWS ITEMS

The Queen announced her New Year's Honours list.
It included 17 Knights and one Dame. The Deputy Prime Minister, John (Black Jack) McEwen was honoured. So too was Newspaper baron, **Frank Packer**. His award was not related to his business activities, but rather for **his services to Australian and international yachting**....

Packer was later very much involved in **Australia's efforts to win the America's Cup**. He sponsored Gretel and Gretel II, unsuccessful in 1962 and 1970. His first wife's was named Gretel....

Actor Chips Rafferty, and the British writer Agatha Christie, were also honoured.

The first **divorce in Italy** in modern times was granted

.One front-page headline on January 1st read "Biggest Australian ambush kills 21 Vietcong." **This was typical,** every day. Sometimes the numbers killed were much bigger, sometimes there were several such reports in a day. **Sometimes it was our own and American troops who were victims**....

But I remind you that a war was going on, and that men were being killed. I will not take up my pages by reporting battles every day. Instead, **I will report on the war only when something special happens. But keep in mind that disasters were happening every day**, and that our own military forces were bearing the brunt of it all.

A 21-year-old girl, Penny Plemmer, was to marry at a small city on NSW Central Coast. Parents expected about 50 people to attend. But **500 locals turned up** and crowded out the church and spilled over into the road....

The reason was that the beautiful Penny had recently **held the Miss World title for a year**, and the locals were justly proud of her. When asked about her future, Penny said "**I just want to be a housewife**", much to the annoyance of the **growing** feminist movement.

66 soccer fans were killed in Glasgow at the end of a match. People leaving the ground before the final whistle turned back in when they heard the clamour from a late goal. People were either trampled to death, or were suffocated as they tumbled down steps onto those below.

A maritime strike in Greece had our local sea-front workers all steamed up. So when a Greek ship arrived in Sydney, they refused to work on it. That meant that it was moored in the Harbour, and the passengers had to be brought ashore in small lifeboats....

320 passengers had to thus disembark, and **650** embarked in return. The loading operation took over eight hours to complete....

This was a period when strikers had much leeway. Union oganisers were constantly using their Trade Union power to **dislocate normal functioning of society** with all sorts of petty issues. **This strike over an industrial matter in Greece** illustrates how silly our world had become.

SOME HINTS FOR THE YEAR AHEAD

At times, as I am writing these books, I watch as the years roll by, and I despair. I see matters that are just plain wrong that are crying out for reform, and yet no one does anything about them But sometimes, I can see movement, and progress towards a better state of affairs.

Right now, at the start of 1971, I can see four trends that came out of the sixties where long-term change will soon enough result in a different aspect for society.

I describe them briefly them below. I add, **I think** that these will result in a better world. But I know that change is not always for the better, and I leave it to the reader now in the 2020's to decide whether the world has improved much.

COMMUNITY ORGANISATION

In 1960, if persons had a complaint against some development in the community, they could create **a local fuss,** and write Letters to editors. The papers were full of these. In most cases they made no difference at all.

With the sixties came the realisation that hard-minded entrepreneurs and policy makers would never be swayed by **scattered** opposition. But, it became clear, they **would** listen to **organisations** of these opponents who persuaded them using multiple arguments.

Hence, the trend I am talking about, the nature of counter-attacks changed, from a multitude of individuals to larger representative groups. National bodies were set up, national conferences were organised, secretariats were established. In other words, the community of objectors got their acts together, and the big end of town found that issues affecting the environment were matters for reasoned debate with worthy opponents of equal size.

As you all know, environmental provisions now play a really big role in many decisions. An impact study is needed for **all** building proposals, and the fate of the red-boned sea-gull often dominates our News outlets for days.

Whether this reality is good news is open to argument. Has the swing gone too far, and will good projects be delayed for years, or abandoned, because of sea-gulls? Or can anyone justify the wiping out of rare gulls just for the profit of a few?

I do not try to answer such questions. Instead, I simply point out that the defiant attitudes that fostered the objections in the Sixties were still there, and growing at the start of the Seventies, and we could expect to hear more of this as we progress **through this book.**

DECLINING INFLUENCE OF THE CHURCHES

In WWII, the Christian Churches had plenty to offer those millions of ordinary people who were suffering anguish over the fate of their menfolk. After the war, the world became much better educated, and the general diffusion of science in particular challenged the basis of Christian beliefs.

Since then, religion has suffered a gradual decline in its penetration into society. For example, the growing incidence of divorce undermined the sanctity of a basic pillar for religion. The widespread acceptance of the Pill meant that many women, especially Catholics, were torn from their Churches. The general acceptance of different moral standards accelerated the drift from organised religion, and the failure of clergy to respond in a meaningful way added further to it.

The Churches in various ways did try to fight back. For example, they tried to become more ecumenical, and reduced their petty bickering between the Churches, but only somewhat. On a different tack, Billy Graham brought two of his Crusades to this nation, and for a moment, re-engaged a million faithful. But their efforts have not born permanent fruit, and the statistics for Church attendance and other measures continue to fall.

Importantly, the voices of the Church hierarchy, once deemed so very important, are scarcely heard when our leaders consider affairs of State.

Looking from here, in January 1971, it seems that this drift away from religion will continue unabated.

THE LABOR PARTY RENAISSANCE
Doc Evatt and Arthur Calwell were now gone, and their mind-crippling ideologies that centred around nationalisation of much of the economy, had gone with them. Vast hordes of citizens breathed a deep sigh of relief.

The Liberals, and their allies in the Country Party, were floundering. Their leader for the last 20 years, Bob Menzies, had gone, and his successor, Harold Holt, had drowned in the ocean. John Gorton casually took up the vacant role, and as we will see, looked uncertain on really good days.

So the scene was being set for a political shake-up. It looked like it might come from Labor's Gough Whitlam, the Party's new leader. He was bright-eyed and bushy-tailed and was rampaging through the stuffy and smoky corridors of the remnant old-guard.

Without sticking my neck out too far, I think that this young man might have a future in politics, and might even shake things up quite a lot.

OUR INVOLVEMENT IN VIETNAM

Support for the Vietnam war was dropping fast in the US. The scandal over the mass shooting of citizens in Vietnam villages was growing as the US watched such slaughters nightly on their TVs.

About 20 per cent of their troops had been repatriated already, and more were likely soon.

Support for the war was also dropping in Australia. After all, if the Yanks were losing enthusiasm for **their** war, it was hard to whip up enthusiasm for it here.

But behind that was the gradual realisation that the war was pointless. Neither side would ever claim a victory, the initial goals were forgotten, and the whole conflict was bogged down with talks of this and that treaty, or ceasefire, with the parties getting further and further apart as they reflected on their accumulating grievances.

Logic said bring the boys home, and that might just be on the cards.

MERINO RAM EMBARGO

Australia still earned much of its overseas money from its sales of wool. As a spin off from that, it also was in a position to earn small fortunes from the sales of its merino rams for breeding.

These rams had come from Spain 200 years ago, and had been carefully bred so that now they were magnificent animals that produced wonderful progeny. They were the wonder of the sheep world.

It was often suggested that we as a nation should export some of these to other countries for a handsome profit. The counter argument was that if we did so, competitors in other nations would develop top quality wool, and then undercut us in world markets.

These arguments had waxed and waned for over a decade, and no one policy or view had dominated. The Letter below represents the current state of play.

Letters, G Killen. According to reports, the Minister for Primary Industry, Mr Anthony, has now to consider whether the government should accept advice of the Australian Wool Industry Conference to extend further the lifting of the merino ram embargo.

Mr Anthony, on the advice of this non-elected "conference," used administrative powers to lift the 40-year embargo early last year. The question was not debated in Parliament and no debate has since been permitted. Australia's merino competitors were given access to our best sires with which to improve the quality and quantity of their production.

Some of our self-interested stud breeders, wool professors and scientists had led us to believe there would be little demand for our rams. Events have shown how inaccurate these arguments were. Some 211 merino rams were bought at auction for such low-wage countries as Africa, the Argentine Republic, China, India and the Soviet Union. These countries can produce wool well below our cost-inflation affected levels.

The Soviet Union alone has bought 136 rams and its representative at the sale told our breeders that Russia wants to increase its quantity of merino wool by injection of stronger, heavier-fleeced types.

The Australian woolgrower is fighting his greatest battle ever to stay in the industry during a period of lowered demand. During the last 12 months, he has come to realise just how wrong was the advice given that wool's problem was world under-production.

The embargo issue, like others, has divided industry spokesmen. But its deep impact on country voters was shown in the recent Senate elections when a great Country Party stalwart in Senator Tom Bull lost his seat. Many other Liberal and Country Party members have become aware of the dissatisfaction of country voters with the Government's action.

The New South Wales Graziers' Association and the United Farmers and Woolgrowers' Association of New South Wales are a great deal more representative of the views of woolgrowers in this great wool State than the so-called Wool Industry Conference. Both bodies have expressed strong opposition to the lifting of the ban, and warned of damage to the industry.

Regardless of any argument with the trade-union movement, it would be absolutely wrong for the Federal Government to preside over a further extension of the embargo to the advantage of Australia's competitors.

OZ CRICKET IN STRIFE

At the moment, the English cricket team was touring Australia and giving us a hiding. Whenever this happens, attendances at Tests are always down, there is a lot of criticism of the Captaincy, and everyone looks round for a scapegoat, often the Selectors.

At the same time, Letter writers talk about the changes that need to be made to make the game better, or to draw bigger crowds, or to provide brighter cricket. The truth is that none of these are ever adopted, and the grand game goes on unaffected.

At the moment, cricket lovers in Oz are being slowly tortured, so any bright idea for change gets a bit of Press space.

Letters, S Bellmaine. International cricket is declining in popularity and people are discussing the chances of arresting this decline. Here is a suggestion:

During the tour of a visiting team, let there be five "Tests of cricket," each "Test of cricket" to consist of a double event:-

(a) A single innings match, no time limit, played to the finish; for the winners - two points.

(b) A so-called "knock-out" one-day match (similar to the recent successful match in Melbourne) with 40 overs only for each side; for the winners - one point.

The whole series would thus be decided on the best of 15 points. There could be no such result as a drawn series.

The one-day "knock-out" match could be played either immediately following the other match or it could be programmed for "prime viewing time", say the Sunday, even if this meant the interruption of the other match.

Those who appreciate "traditional cricket" would find that some of its virtues had been retained; those who desire action and the certainty of a result would see these attained.

The whole scheme would be a significant departure from traditional cricket; there are many sports-lovers who think that a departure is necessary.

Comment. I am sure that the authorities at the time ignored this Letter, as it did the others. But it does contain the germ of one-day and 40-overs cricket that have now, in the years 2020-plus, become so popular in the Cricket Calender.

CRITICISM OF ROYALTY

Ten years ago, Prince Philip and the young Prince Charles went shooting in India, and were proudly able to display a dead tiger that they had shot. There was no criticism at the time.

But look at the correspondence now.

Letters, Mira Kramer. A few weeks ago, Prince Philip helped to raise 4,000,000 Pounds for his pet charity, the World Wildlife Fund.

Last week he achieved another distinction, when he and Prince Charles killed about 300 pheasants in the first shoot of 1971 at Sandringham.

As a bystander who is following Prince Philip's vigorous save-the-animals campaign, I would like an honest answer to this question: Is Prince Philip fighting for the preservation of world animals because he loves them or because he wants more targets to shoot at?

Letters, A Bowie. I read in your paper the Letter from a lady complaining about Prince Philip shooting pheasants. She is obviously a nature-lover and was criticising Prince Philip, who also poses as a nature-lover.

Perhaps this lady does not realise that pheasants in Britain and other European countries are largely reared as a food product, and when hatched are carefully tended until old enough to fend for themselves. They are turned loose as a rule in woods adjacent to big estates.

All of those 300 shot pheasants mentioned would have been sold in various markets and purchased by individual families who prefer a pheasant to a chicken, as I do myself. After all, this lady probably enjoys roast chicken as much as I do, unless she is a complete vegetarian; in which case, of course, she would never touch meat or meat extracts, or anything in that nature, and this would include milk and cream (as it would be robbing the calf of its natural food).

I am also a nature-lover, but reason must prevail, and to run the Prince down in this manner is very unfair and might convey a totally erroneous impression to the public in general.

Comment. Over the decade, the attitude in Britain and Australia had changed somewhat. Granted, most people here still supported that Monarchy and, for example, Royal Tours to Australia still attracted huge crowds and dozens of fainting schoolgirls.

But there were signs that criticism of Royalty, previously sacred, was allowed, provided it was moderate and about smaller matters. There was not as yet any sign of a Republican aggression that emerged 20 years later. But still, times were changing, and a few people were thinking that the position of the monarchy might change as well.

A NEW WAY OF RAISING REVENUE
Councils, like every other governmental body, always needed more money to provide the services they offer or

want to offer. So they were ready at all times to use their ingenuity to create a new revenue stream. This was at a time when the new creed, **Make the User Pay,** was coming into vogue.

Letters, S Berg. I drove to Mona Vale tip the other day to dump some accumulated rubbish. I was greatly surprised to be stopped by a collector - complete with new money satchel and folder of tickets - who demanded 10c before letting me in.

As this was a new "hold up," I objected, but was told that, from now on, all would have to pay to enter the tip.

After I had handed over my 10c, he added if I had a Shire sticker I could go in free. Unfortunately, I don't like to adorn my car with stickers, but I informed him I was a resident of Collaroy, and had been for some time. But no sticker, no go.

The collector was no doubt acting under instructions, but it strikes me as rather incongruous that at a time when we are all exhorted to be tidy and prevent pollution, an entrance fee should be charged for dumping one's rubbish where rubbish should be dumped.

Comment. Of course, by the 2020's, the payment of fees to dump rubbish has been universally accepted, if not without resentment by some oldies. So too has the idea that the **user pays** extra for all sorts of services, even though often the user has already paid through taxes or charges.

Life's like that.

SOMETHING FOR BIRD-LOVERS

Letters, Joan Sherwood. Re Churchill, the month-old swimming pigeon, I wonder how many other people find birds taking a dip in the backyard pool.

For some years we have had the pleasure of the company of a black and white peewit who at a tender age lost a leg. He has become so tame he daily hops around for food scraps thrown to him by the children and then he, too, has his dip in the pool. He will do so even when the children are in the pool. Then he sits on the rim to flutter his wings free of water and preen himself.

This is marvellous for the children, as it teaches them to treat wild creatures with care and allows them to observe them at close range.

BRAVE OR FOOLISH?

Three Victorian **canoeists attempting to cross the Bass Straight** are expected to arrive within a day.

FEBRUARY NEWS ITEMS

There is **no Government ban on the export of merinos**, but **there is a Trade Union ban**. So, an enterprising pilot has been **flying the sheep out to Fiji**, four at a time....

The Union movement is cranky about this, and the Feds are shy about discussing it. **Eleven flights have been made so far**, but the pilot's only worry was that the grazing industry would buy its own aircraft. That would cut him out of the act.

But **the merino war hotted up next day**. A Melbourne Export Marketing Company had hired a Boeing 720 to fly 150 rams to Russia. The ACTU, the leading Trade Union body in Australia, refused to fuel the plane, and **declared the shipment "Black"**....

Two days later, the rams were taken to the Air Force base at Sydney's Richmond, and were flown out in a different Boeing. This plane had been re-fueled by Air Force personnel, and was not subject to Trade Union Rules....

All of this was done on an order by the Prime Minister, John Gorton, who was determined that Union activity would not interfere with Australia's business commitments. The Unions by now were very cranky.

John Anderson was elected as Leader of the Country Party. This Party was in a coalition with the ruling Liberal Party, and could be relied on to support the

Government. He was a non-controversial figure, and gave solid support over many years.

Do you remember Edgar Mitchell? Of course you don't. What about **Alan Shepard**?

Well, they were the two US astronauts who **landed on the moon on February 5th**. This was **the second moon walk**, but it was still novel enough to thrill the US, and many other people around the world. They will mainly collect rock samples, and stay there for 30 hours.

Jim Kennedy of Brisbane has sorted out **his problem over his phone bill**. He had noticed that the bill for **trunk calls last April was suspiciously high**. The various authorities investigated, and found that when **the Queen visited Brisbane last April**, her phone calls to Buckingham Palace were mistakenly charged to Kennedy's account....

A total of 25 minutes was involved, and he was happy to pay it for the Queen. However, **the bill will be paid by Prime Minister's Department.** Mr Kennedy hopes that the Queen might now make him "**Baron Kennedy of Breakfast Creek.**" This has not yet happened.

Sutherland Shire Council is on the NSW coast, with good beaches. A visiting South African surfing team **applied for Council's permission to play** a sporting "Test" against local surfers. The Council rejected the application because **the team was all white.** This was **the first local Council in Australia to declare opposition to Apartheid**.

A NEW PORTFOLIO

Our Australian Governmental system is very stable. Since Federation in 1901, and before, we have seen most of the Houses and Senates, and Upper and Lower Chambers serve their full term without revolutions, riots and crippling strikes. By contrast, in many nations, for example Italy, governments have changed every few months. And there is a multitude of countries in South America and Africa that are just as worthy of mention.

This stability means that our national policies can be developed and carried through. This has been good for the nation, and we should all rejoice in that. But, it makes also for a form of monotony, things go on and on for years without disruption, and the pace of change is slow.

So, when a few politicians in NSW said that, if elected, they would introduce a new Portfolio into their Ministry, people got excited. When these politicians added that the new Ministry would be in matters pertaining to Sports and Recreation, more people got even more excited.

The point was that many people thought that sports were private and personal matters, that sportsmen played for their own satisfaction, and they felt that a new Ministry would see the long arm of Government take all the enjoyment out of sport, and its administration.

But there were supporters of this new idea.

Letters, (Dr) John Bloomfield, Physical Education, University of Western Australia. As one interested in "the conservation of man," I heartily applaud the recent announcement by the Premier of NSW, Mr Askin, of the proposed formation of a Ministry of Sport.

His Government, in making the first move in this direction in Australia, is catering for a sorely needed organisation which will encourage and promote sport and recreation in his State.

There may well be some critics who will maintain that such a Government body is not warranted at this time, and that Australians are a fit and healthy nation.

Statistics gathered over the last five years, however, show that at present 55 per cent of deaths in Australia are due to cardiovascular disease, and that Australia now has the third highest incidence of this degenerative disease in the world.

The increase of cardiovascular diseases is most marked in young and middle-aged men. In addition, rejection rates of young men for National Service are now up to 44 per cent, and results of standard medical tests are poor when compared to figures taken during World War II, or the National Service period of the 1950s. Moreover, the life expectancy of the Australian male is considerably less than that of his European counterpart, and is decreasing each year, whereas it is steadily increasing in Europe.

The above problems have mainly occurred because of increasing urbanisation and the automation of our daily existence. Previously, man has been forced to have physical activity in order to stay alive.

More than 20 European countries now have ministries of recreation and sport. Australia is one of the only remaining Western countries which does not have such an organisation.

This step, then, by the Government of NSW, is a monumental one in catering for the future physical well-being of Australians from the preventive medical point of view. It should be strongly supported by all interested in the physical welfare of man.

There were, however, many who opposed the concept. Below is just one Letter from a myriad that followed.

Letters, R Blake. The announcement that Mr Askin or Mr Hills, if elected, will create a Ministry of Sport, complete with Cabinet minister, caused me first incredulous wonder, followed quickly by hysterical hilarity. I am now gravely concerned - they are serious!

Both these gentlemen have assailed our ears, in chorus with many other learned experts, with warnings that we are in an inflationary situation which, without great care and public sacrifice, will become a national disaster. Both these gentlemen, on many occasions have complained that the State is bankrupt, that there is not enough money made available from Canberra for various essential requirements such as education, hospitals, the police force etc.

If these claims are correct, how can we justify the increased expenditure automatically associated with any new ministerial department? How can we expect such frivolous behaviour to influence the Commonwealth Government to loosen the purse strings?

I predict that Sir Henry Bolte must be rubbing his hands with glee and composing telegrams expressing a desire to meet our new Minister of Sport and his inevitable director-of-indoor-games. Sir Henry undoubtedly could use this as proof positive that Victoria needs much more Commonwealth assistance than NSW.

After all, which State is rich enough to support a Ministry of Sport?

Comment. You all know where this battle has gotten to. Today, our vast Olympic teams are financed by the Government, with all sorts of training and performance perks, fully funded by the Government. Almost every sport has its own Institute with grand national headquarters, often in many States. The new sporting Clubs are government financed, and they have their own centralised inspectors, who take delight in finding breaches of the National Codes.

In short, the old concept of sport for pleasure has often given way to the idea of sports for business and profit. The playing of tennis on a Saturday afternoon is rarely seen. The schoolboy kicking of a footy on a paddock has given way to jumpers and uniforms, and twenty organised games on a Saturday morning with lots of Mums watching on.

Swimmers with ambition spend half their lives with their faces under water as they do endless laps of the pool.

And they start doing this at about age six, and do it for a decade or more. There is something to be said for grabbing a towel and saying "let's go for a swim".

Second comment. Despite the nostalgic way the above paragraphs came out, please do not brand me as anti-change. I can also describe many pleasures that come from the newer forms of sports organisations. For example, our youth are better instructed, and the capacity for injury is greatly reduced.

In any case, Government-financed sport now satisfies many Australians. Teams and Clubs get grants for facilities, playing fields, club-houses, travel, uniforms, staging events, and all sorts of things. **It all started** because a couple of politicians in 1971 timidly suggested that Government support was a good thing. **They** thought that. What do **you** think?

YOUNG WOMEN ON A ROLL

In the Forties and Fifties, most young people had some experience with roller skates. They offered the thrill of rapid transit from one place to another, as well as the bruises and scratches that once filled all young lives. But they had limited practical use in this unpaved nation, so they were used mainly by boys in shopping strips to annoy and terrorise the oldies.

However, in the US, around 1962, a new form of sport developed that grew into what was called Roller Derbies. This had teams of mainly girls racing round an indoor track with the aim of getting to the end-point with more points gained than the opposition.

Over a few years, as the popularity of the sport increased, it started to attract larger audiences, especially on TV. It also developed internationally, and World Cups came into being. It flowed to Australia, and as more and more arenas were built where the girls could practise and compete, the fun of watching the sport on TV attracted many viewers.

But as the sport developed, over the next decade, it got rougher and rougher. The idea of pretty American girls with blond pony tails gave way to lumpy viragoes with pointy elbows and crash tackles. In America, there were dozens of casualties as the players were bounced over side-rails and as hosts of them were kicked and squashed and head-high tackled.

In Australia, outrage among mothers grew and grew. This was violence in the home, on their own settees, with their daughters lapping it up and cheering blow by blow. Their cute and precious little darlings were cheering as their American counter-parts maimed and assaulted each other. For the mums, this became too much to tolerate.

The Christian Churches became vocal against the roller cult. Mothers en masse wrote Letters to Editors expressing their horror For months on end, they deplored the entire roller game sport and swore some type of retaliation,

Letters, Petra Power. I have no need to describe the brutality that one sees every week in the Roller Derby. Everyone is familiar with the dreadful display of violence that is exploiting and corrupting young girls across the nation.

Instead, I am writing to inform you that we mothers on the Sydney North Shore are forming a Committee that will boycott your paper if you continue to give favourable support to the mayhem, through your columns. Further, if you continue, we will boycott the Companies that continue to advertise through your Paper.

It is a fact that, though this Committee was formed just a week ago, we have already over 200 mothers and fathers who are as anxious as I am about the unmitigated violence that can be seen every week on TV.

We urge you to stop the reports immediately.

At the same time, a more dignified form of roller skating was also in difficulties. Here there was none of the hysteria of Roller Game. It was sedate, well managed and respectable. One writer described it as "Ballroom dancing on wheels." Another said it was "effete". In any case, there no large crowds of spectators, and no TV extolling the brutality of muggers. But the **same brush** that was tarring Roller Game **was being felt by this form of family recreation.**

Its demise is lamented below.

Letters, P Tannenbaum. In the plight of the Australian Roller Skating Club to save the last roller rink in Sydney, I believe a few significant facts about the sport of roller skating have been overlooked.

The first of these is that roller skating, like ice skating, is an international competitive sport which requires great skill. The present areas of international competition include men's free skating, ladies' free skating, pairs dance skating, pairs free skating, speed skating and roller hockey.

This year, the Australian and Pacific roller-skating championships will be held in Brisbane, and the world skating championships will be in Spain.

In its true character, a skating rink is a place where the children can be left for the day, where young people can go for enjoyment or even dates, and where parents can go with (or without) their children.

The last point is that organised skating in Australia is barely 10 years old and is already fighting to maintain its true character. In 1968 Australia entered a world championship event for the first time with a team of four art skaters, but how many people knew of this?

If skating is allowed to become extinct in Sydney, Australia will lose another link in one of the most popular participation sports in the world.

Comment. The US Roller Derby went bust in the US in 1972, mainly because of protests like the one above. It re-started in 1978, and the Rules and controls were gradually improved so that by turn of the Century, it had regained a decent following.

Since then, it has continued to grow in all nations, and by the early 2020's there are a hundred local clubs in Australia, and some of these participate in world events and Test Matches. Much of the violence has been removed from the sport, the referees are better, the protective gear has improved, and so the injury toll has reduced greatly. In short, the game has become more civilised **and so, probably, the mass appeal has faded**.

Still, it carries vestiges of the past. Players' shirts still carry the stage name of the players. "Bloody Mary", "Roving Revenger", and "May Hem" still go round the track. And they play for the "Rampant   Hatchets", and the "Kiki Kapows", and the "Outside Main Streamers."

As for the "ballroom" roller skaters, I can find no evidence of their renaissance. I have no doubt that it still exists somewhere, but like ballroom dancing itself, it would only be a small shadow of its former self.

Footnote. Roller Derby skating has always been the domain of younger girls. The boys currently get a go, but the attention has stayed on the girls.

TRADE UNIONS STILL ACTIVE

I remind you that the battle over sheep exports was still going on. Shipments of live merinos were getting out of the country by various devices, and that was good news for the Government and the graziers. But the Unions were very much opposed to this, and were doing all they could to stop the sheep moving to greener pastures.

The Unions were also active in lots of other matters. They were becoming a powerful force acting within the tempestuous Labor Party. And they were at odds with the advancing Right wing of the Party, and were certainly much at odds with the general population. But, at the moment, they had plenty of power to disrupt the lives of ordinary people, and they exercised that power liberally.

Letters, J Nicholson. Who runs this country - the Government or the unions?

The facts are clear - the unions decide that rams can't be exported, they refuse to load ships for Greece, they refuse to pay fines for breaches of the law, they threaten strikes if legal action is taken against any union official, they propose action to force the Government's hand on social issues, they decide whether the community will be allowed to receive mail, petrol, community services, etc., almost ad infinitum.

There can be no doubt as to the facts - the unions, not the Government, run the country.

The answer is simple. In a democratic country we are given the right to elect our representatives at the ballot box. The Government should either exercise its authority or give the community **the right to elect the union officials** who control our lives.

Comment. At the moment, the Liberal Party was in Government, but it too was in turmoil after the resignation of Bob Menzies, and the disappearance of Harold Holt. Even if the Party wanted to take on the Unions, it was not politically strong enough, at the time, to do this.

NOISE POLLUTION

The environment was becoming a popular matter to complain about. I mentioned earlier that people were forming organised groups and starting movements to fight for environmental issues.

But the definition of the problem was also changing. From the fifties, young people with transistor radios had haunted solace seekers on public transport and beaches and from across the street. A few years later, hotels with the new 10 o'clock closing, and their noise fests into the night, irritated neighbours.

By 1971, defenders of a quiet life were on the war-path against what was now being called "noise pollution." In the cities, complaints were being made about low-flying aircraft near the flight paths, and about the times at which planes could land.

The Letter belows shows some of the growing animosity to noise making.

Letters, P Smith. A political party that is prepared to make the elimination of noise a plank of reform in these coming elections will have the votes of many, many thousands.

Mr Hills has given a hint, Mr Askin nothing.

What a hell for the public to have to put up with almost every day and every night! Noises emanating from the slamming of car doors, the revving of engines, exhausts (if any, worn out, or useless), huge trucks, parlour cars, buses, drivers having not the slightest regard for the public.

Surely noises can be controlled or moderated. Noise is a killer, a long-range killer, destroying the nervous system by degrees. What about a minister with responsibility to eliminate this evil?

Letters, Tess Van Sommers. Mr Smith mentions only traffic noise.

Until the internal combustion engine is replaced by something like the fuel cell, we are stuck with traffic noise. There is, however, another form of noise, totally unnecessary and just as injurious as traffic din, that could be legally controlled - and nobody would suffer, economically or otherwise.

This is the noise of music and entertainment machines of all kinds that now batters people in built-up areas from all sides, sometimes 18 hours and more in the 24.

Popular music is now played by decibel addicts so loudly that even closed doors and windows will not contain or shut out the sound of it, and it can intrude hundreds of yards from its source.

Can anyone tell me what right any person has to force me to listen to music not of my own choosing? To do this to me is surely to commit trespass and assault upon me, and to pollute my environment.

If I let even my harmless dog stray on my neighbour's premises, throw rubbish into his grounds or stones at his windows, he has immediate redress against me through the authorities.

Yet he can destroy my peace of mind in my own home, and wreck my nervous health, by assaulting me with the loud noises he finds pleasurable, and my only redress is an expensive civil suit.

In civilised communities (eg Britain, France) there are laws to stop people making a nuisance of themselves to their neighbours with loud music.

Why must we suffer, virtually unprotected, from what I would dub the "noiseniks"?

Comment. Things have gotten worse, I think. The worst experience I can have is to go to a party or a wedding or just a restaurant and find that shouting is needed to utter a single word. Of course, youth concerts would be worse, but I don't go to many of these nowadays.

CUTS IN VIETNAM
Australian forces in November last year numbered about 10,000. In that month, a whole Battalion of 3,000 men was returned home. Now the Army has indicated that a further 700 men will also be released.

This is consistent with the fall in support for the war that the nation was experiencing. But still, internally, the arguments and demonstrations went on, and the whole affair was such that no one mentioned it unless they wanted a fight.

THE MERINO BAN STILL
I will not go into detail, except to mention that the merino issue was still on the table for argument.

The Letter below gives you an indication of that. Don't worry about the detail, just note that all parties to the issue are still very vocal, and showing no signs of a settlement.

Letters, D McClelland, ALP Senator for NSW. By ordering the RAAF to service a civilian aircraft to fly merino rams out of Australia, the Government is completely ignoring and holding in contempt the expressed opinion of the Australian Senate.

In April, 1969, after a full-scale debate and by majority vote, the Senate expressed the opinion that the embargo on the export of merinos should not be removed at that time. **And** that the embargo should remain in force until a majority of those persons affected shall decide by referendum or other means in favour of removing or relaxing the embargo.

The senators who voted for the decision in fact represented a majority of Australian electors.

MARCH NEWS ITEM

A lion called Amber **grabbed his keeper at Cairo zoo** yesterday, **tore him apart, and ate him** while horrified visitors watched and fainted.

Thirteen girl hairdressers in Victoria's country town of Warrugal **have applied for a cut in wages** so that they can keep their jobs. They say that they are amazed at the 24 per cent increases in their wages since December 1969. They said the salon had increased prices and the number of customers had fallen constantly....

Their application went to the State Minster for Labour, who said he was not able to **reduce** wages. He suggested that they try the Wages Board, but that Board said, after consideration, that **it too could not help**....

The girls so far are forced to accept their higher pay.

In Victoria, more than 100 motorists have **been booked by police for failing to wear seat belts. New regulations** enforcing their wearing will come into effect in most other States within a few months.

Sean Connery had given up his job as 007 because he got bored. Now, however, **he has relented** and will be back with *"Diamonds are Forever."* His fee will go to the Scottish International Development Trust.

A Texas jury took 60 minutes to **sentence a man to 1,800 years imprisonment** for drug pushing....

Oddly, he will be eligible for parole in 20 years. **Only in America.**

The World Heavyweight fight, between the current Title Holder Joe Frazier and the **challenger Mohamed Ali (Cassius Clay)**, will be televised live in Sydney and Melbourne. The fight will have a world record audience of 300 million viewers, and will be scheduled for 15 rounds. Frazier will be a slight favourite against resurgent Ali....

This was at a time **when boxing was still held in high repute**, and hence was of great interest to everyday Australians. Since then **management and control of the fight industry has been scattered**, with multiple boxers claiming to be the champion, in every weight class. Can you guess **who won?**

The East Malvern Branch of a Melbourne Bank has been closed because it has **been help-up by armed gunmen five times in three years.** All of the eastern States of the nation are suffering from similar hold-ups.

In Melbourne, two men were each jailed for six years for importing drugs into Australia and arranging for their sale. 60,000 tablets were involved and were smuggled into the country in camera cases. **The drugs were hallucinogenic** and were new to Australia. They are known by **the shortened name as LSD.** It is feared that their use in Australia **could** become more widespread.

You were (nearly) all wrong. The bout went for 15 rounds, and then all three judges gave it to Frasier on points. **Clay was badly battered**, and there is currently speculation about **whether he will fight again.**

CHANGING OF THE GUARD

The Liberal Party, backed by the Country Party, held the reins of power in Canberra. It had an uncomfortably small majority in the House, and this was reduced to about four Members at the moment because of illness. So, the leaders were looking over their shoulders for any signs of dissension in their ranks.

About March 5th, some of this dissension started to boil up. Malcolm Fraser, the Minister for Defence, began objecting about the way the Prime Minister, John Gorton, was handling certain matters relating to Defence, especially in Vietnam. Fraser rattled round for a few days, and then resigned as Minister.

This called into open question Gorton's handling of matters, and it was quite clear that Fraser was about to challenge Gorton for leadership of the Liberal Party. A few other Liberals thought that they might also have a chance if a spill occurred, so they held up their hands for supporters, and canvassed the ranks.

Needless to say, for about a week, the Press was gloating over the orgy of charge and counter-charge that all these factions provided. At the same time, the Labor Party rejoiced in the turmoil, as the general public wondered if the Liberals were fit to run the country, given that they could scarcely run their own Party.

By March 10th, decisions were made. In a meeting of the Liberal Party, Gorton was challenged by the dark-horse, William McMahon. The vote was tied, so that left the final vote, the decision, in the hands of the Chair of the meeting, John Gorton.

He decided to vote, not for himself, but for McMahon. Though he was not fully done yet, because he was voted to become the Deputy Leader of the Party.

McMahon then automatically became Prime Minister, and as usual, said he would make changes to policy and personnel. It seems that one defeated challenger, Malcolm Fraser, would be re-admitted to Cabinet, and thus remain a key person in the Government.

It could well be that we will hear more from Mr Fraser.

SMH **Editorial.** The Liberal Party chose as its leader the one man who has the stature to restore unity to the Party and to set the Government on a stable course. As Mr Gorton's light has waned, Mr McMahon's has waxed. He still has his critics and detractors, but the steady courage he has shown in a very awkward political situation has diminished them. His political skill, his adaptability, his quick and able mind and his long and varied experience qualify him for leadership and should ensure that he avoids the mistakes of his predecessor.

He went on to say that the Liberals would succeed only if they gave up any semblance of division. He applauded Gorton for his sensible decision to recuse himself.

With the best will in the world, Mr McMahon can hardly avoid the feeling that he is walking something of a political tightrope. There will be a temptation to allow too much weight to the factions in the choice of his Cabinet. It is a temptation which, for his own sake no less than the country's sake and the party's sake, he would do well to resist. Nothing would do more to restore public confidence than the demonstration that he had chosen the best men available regardless of their previous affiliations.

Mr McMahon first task is to rally the government and get on with the business of governing Australia which has recently taken second place to internecine party warfare.

Comment. I met **John Gorton** twice. Both meetings were at cocktail parties for International Conferences of Biometricians. He, like most people, had no idea of what a biometrician was. But at the second meeting, surrounded by 1,000 party goers, he cornered me and asked me to tell him all about them and what they did.

He didn't need to do that. There was no political gain to be had from the biometrician vote. He did it because he was interested. I found him to be intelligent, honest, and forthright.

I got the idea that he was not so ambitious that he wanted to be Prime Minister. Now, in 1971, I was not surprised by his own decision to leave the job of PM.

But, he had his detractors.

Letters, W Graham. H Ahern does himself little credit in charging that the Liberal Party moved towards socialism under Mr Gorton's leadership.

Apparently Mr Ahern hasn't heard of the Australian National Line or of TAA and Qantas Airways, all of which are operated by the government in direct competition with private enterprise. The State brickworks and the State abattoir are two more examples of Government enterprise in competition with private enterprise.

In regard to socialisation of distribution, mentioned as part of Labor Party policy by Mr Ahern: if the control exercised over the distribution of primary produce by the multitude of marketing boards and the like doesn't constitute a form of socialisation, I don't know what does.

Is Mr Gorton to blame for all this? Of course not. It all started long before he became Prime Minister, and none of his Liberal predecessors saw fit to change it.

The fact is that while the Liberal and Labor Parties are theoretically far apart, they are in reality forced closer towards one another by the necessity to attract as wide a segment of the electorate as possible.

Letters, M Hart, West New Britain. As an expatriate Australian living in Papua-New Guinea, I have followed with intense interest the Australian political scene of the past fortnight.

An amazing thing happened: Australian politics became overseas news headlines overnight, possibly for the first time in the history of the country.

Whatever else Mr Gorton has or has not done, he must be congratulated for making Australian politics controversial and of great interest to Mr and Mrs Citizen.

Billy McMahon was ambitious. He had been Treasurer for the last few years, and had done a thorough job. The general concensus of opinions is that he was elected because he represented the conservative forces among the Liberals, and that steady, reflective government was needed to combat a charging Gough Whitlam and the Labor Party.

The change of leadership stirred **the general population** very little. Editors published very few Letters about it, and these were clearly from Party hacks who stuck to their pre-birth ideas through thick and thin. Scarcely anyone, outside Canberra, got very excited.

The Labor Party hoped that this Liberal Party fighting would go on forever. They could see in the polls that, after 22 years of continuous rule, the Liberal Party was staggering. On top of that, Geoff Whitlam was figuratively emptying the spitoons at smoke-filled Labor Headquarters around the nation. The "36 faceless men" who had dominated Labor's policy for years were on their way out as he thought new thoughts.

He rejected the 50-year lusting for socialism, nationalisation, price-controls and regulations that the Old Guard longed for. In their stead, he was winning great support for a Labor Party that was concerned with social issues, issues that affected the everyday life of people everywhere.

The fighting within the Liberal ranks, and the prospect of it continuing into the elections next year, was Pennies from Heaven for Labor.

COMMENTS FROM POLITICAL LEADERS

Mr Malcolm Fraser: This man, Gorton, because of his unreasoned drive to get his own way, his obstinacy, his impetuous and emotional reactions, has imposed strains of the Liberal Party, the Government and the Public Service.

Mr Gorton: I feel like a galley slave who has been set free.

Mr McMahon: I don't feel the slightest bit excited or emotional.

Mr Whitlam: I would think Mr McMahon will get on as well with his new deputy as that deputy got on with him as a leader.

Sir Robert Menzies: Having got out of politics five years ago, I desire nothing more than to be left to my retirement.

BOB HAWKE STRIKES A BARGAIN

Many of the major Trade Unions in Australia felt they needed the support of other Unions in their various battles with Corporations and Government. So, over ten years, they had built up a Council to negotiate and do business on their behalf. At the moment, this ACTU, the Australian Council of Trade Unions, had elected Bob Hawke as its President, and he had become its forceful spokesman.

Australia, in the meantime had slowly, over the last decade, legislated to adopt a procedure called Retail Price Maintenance. The RPM, put crudely, meant that a supplier of goods to retailers could set a fixed price and no retailer could sell at any lower price.

Thus, if a retailer wanted to sell the product at a lesser price, he could not do so. That ruled out discounting and it ruled out sales. But it kept the market orderly, and it meant that the producer could be happy that his price would be maintained without disruptive periods of retail price wars.

The argument from suppliers was that if discounting became rife, then the profits of the supplier would drop, and it would be forced out of business.

The ACTU had opened a retail store in Melbourne. It had a wide range of goods, and was just like any other general store. Recently, it decided that it would sell some Dunlop Rubber products at a discount. Dunlop said this was illegal, and Bob Hawke swung into action.

He organised twelve **Unions** to blockade Dunlops. Then he threatened another dozen **retailers** with similar blockades if they did not accept the edict to drop RPM.

Quite a few people thought that these actions were objectionable.

Letters, J Macpherson. The turmoil over confrontation of the ACTU's retail outlet, Bourke's, with Dunlop over resale price maintenance has raised much comment.

While conceding that Mr Hawke does have considerable grounds for his complaints against most forms of RPM, this is a matter which should be left to trade practices legislation. As our present Act does not carry such provisions, Mr Hawke might better direct his energies to securing its inclusion.

A much more important issue arising from this struggle is **the obvious abuse of monopoly power. I refer here not to industries but to unions.**

The ACTU, as recognised leader of the unionist movement in all its activities, occupies the position of monopolist in the labour market and, as such, exerts powers greater than a dozen of the country's largest companies.

Mr Hawke, as ACTU leader, has used his monopolistic power to push Australia's wage rate, or more correctly wage margins, to an absurdly high level and contributes more than anyone else to our alarming cost-push inflation.

He now applies this power in the opposite direction, to attack the manufacturers. He has, in short, told them to accept his prices or else.

Surely these coercive and intimidatory actions come under the arm of our legislation relating to the abuse of monopoly power. The same Trade Practices Act should be brought to bear on this monstrous organisation (more than 20 times the manpower of BHP) to compel it to act in what is vaguely termed the public interest.

One thing is sure: the ACTU has reached far beyond the powers and objectives under which it was formed. Here we have an organisation (or is it just the man?) which through its recent actions shows that it would not hesitate to ruin the entire economy to gain its own ends.

Isn't this why monopoly is a dirty word?

Letters, L Hall. On March 16 on the television program "This Day Tonight" Mr Hawke restated the ACTU policy of opposing the penal strike clauses on the grounds that if suppliers of goods can fix their prices without penalty, **the same should apply to suppliers of labour**.

The statement sounds eminently fair and reasonable, but it completely misses the essential sore point from which the necessity has arisen for control by the Government: The use of industrial sabotage to "sell" labour, as against the lawful, non-disruptive, competitive technique of the sellers of goods, whose main weapon is sales persuasion and who do not really "fix" prices but offer a range of prices, even for the same article in many cases.

The situation is this: We have a commercial community which is a heterogeneous mass of individual businesses, large and small, so loosely organised as a body for any kind of political or other activity that it has neither the desire not the ability to threaten, intimidate, or hold to ransom any other section of the community. It is in fact a pygmy compared with the giant of tightly controlled compulsory unionism, with its power to defy even the elected Government of the country.

For the same reason that our Government allows no person or organisation to have a private army, it cannot and should not tolerate any aggregation of industrial power capable of challenging the power that rightfully belongs to it, the Government.

Letters, H Brink, Managing Director, Nikki Stores. Bond's-Wear Pty Ltd has placed a supply ban on all Nikki Stores since June, 1970, for no other reason than our company's insistence to sell at retail prices some 25 per cent lower than those stipulated by Bond's-Wear.

Since then, Nikki Stores have tried every commercial, legal and political means to have its supplies restored, so far without success.

We have in our possession, however, a letter signed by the Minister for Labour and Industry, Mr Willis, dated March 1, 1971, in which he says:

"The practice of resale price maintenance is not illegal at the present time but the Consumer Affairs Council has recently advised me that it is a practice which is not in the interests of consumers. On the council's recommendations, therefore, I am taking steps to have a thorough investigation made with a view to having the practice outlawed."

The petition our company organised, after the supply ban by Bond's, to have the practice abolished carries now between 20,000 and 30,000 signatures and has received the enthusiastic support of many manufacturers, their agents, staff and many other retailers.

It is clear that an overwhelming proportion of the public and (notwithstanding the public attitude of the Retail Traders' Association) many retailers think it is in the public interest to eradicate the practice utterly and completely. There is no argument in favour of it that can stand up to examination in the clear light of day other than the selfish interest of some companies and some individuals.

Our petition, setting out the reasons why this unfair and abominable practice should be abolished, will be presented shortly to the Prime Minister and to the Premier of New south Wales.

Yet most people agreed that the setting of a fixed price, with no discounting from retailers, was not consistent with our ideas of free enterprise and competition. Their objections were to the method that Hawke used, but not to the outcome he had achieved.

Hawke's approach was clearly blackmail, and all suppliers, including Dunlop, blanched in horror. But within a day, it capitulated and allowed retailers to trade at any price they chose. Other suppliers did likewise over a period of months,and after much to do in the nation's Parliament.

Comment. And that is why, in the 2020's, you can see a retailer's RRP on a product, but he might offer it to you at a lower price. The truth is that it is just that; a **Recommended** price, not a mandated price.

This was just another nail in the coffin of rules and regulations that had carried over since the war.

HELP FOR MUMS

Letters, (Mrs) M Turner. There is a baby boom in Sydney, but I would like to know how other mothers surmount what to me is almost an insoluble problem: what do you do about shopping between the time the baby is born and the time he is able to sit up?

In the suburb where I shop, there are five grocery chain-stores and, in all of them, there is not one shopping trolley in which a baby can be laid down. One store, only just opened, does not even have trolleys in which children can sit.

My husband works on Saturdays, so I have to do my own shopping. With a baby on four-hourly feeds, a three-year-old who starts to get hungry at midday, and two schoolchildren coming home at 3.30pm, my time is limited - and if that one trolley is in use I quite literally cannot shop.

APRIL NEWS ITEMS

Following on from Bob Hawke's threats last month, the Federal Government will introduce measures **to declare Retail Price Maintenance illegal**. Most price fixing is dead. **A good win for Bob. He is a relatively young man with a future. Keep your eye on him.**

Three graziers, who could not make sheep farming pay, instead took to **opal fossicking** for a living. Now, they have found an opal, two inches by 1 inch in size, and **weighing 170 carats**. It will be named the "Orient Queen." **Australia's biggest opal, the "Pride of Australia",** was found in 1919, and weighed 225 carats.

A man in a shop in Kensington High Street in London stole a **five Pound Mickey Mouse kaleidoscope**. He was chased from the shop by assistants, and stopped only when he was crash tackled by a youth....

He was arrested by Police, but it turned out he was **a Second Secretary at the Russian Embassy**. So he had **diplomatic immunity and was released**. Note that even today, diplomatic immunity **is still available to diplomats in Australia. Quaint....**

Do you remember what a kaleidoscope is?

The South African cricket team will visit Australia later this year. The team has already been selected, and **two players have been left out** because the South African Government **will not allow black players in international teams....**

Western Australia and South Australia have banned the visitors. Victoria and NSW are neutral on the issue. Queensland welcomes them with open arms. We will see what they all say when the tour gets closer, and they think about **the revenues lost from the gates.**

Manfred B Lee, the co-author of the famous **Ellery Queen mystery novels,**.has died quietly in America. The authors wrote their first novel in 1928, and continued until Lee's death. Their books, and their TV versions, **entertained two generations.**

Hirohito, Emperor of Japan, held that position during WWII. He was granted an **Order of the Garter in 1929** by King George V. This was the world's most prestigious honour. **He was stripped of it during WWII....**

It has now been granted back to him by a forgiving Queen. There will still be **many in Australia whose hatred of all things Japanese will resent this decision.**

The anti-Vietnam protests still go on. Five Melbourne women disrupted a Department of Labor's meeting to protest against actions affecting their conscripted sons. A magistrate **sentenced each of them to 14 days prison.**

In Melbourne, three former police detectives were found guilty of having perverted the course of justice. They had accepted **bribes to turn a blind eye** to the existence of premises for the performance of abortion. **This practice was still illegal in all Australian States....**

Their trial lasted 47 days, a record in Melbourne's criminal courts..

TOUGH TIMES IN AMERICA

Over that last two years, Americans had become more and more disenchanted with the Vietnam war. At the start, back in about 1964, many Americans had been gung-ho about giving the Reds a dose of medicine, and stopping their insidious drive into South East Asia. But as the death toll rose, and it became obvious that the Vietcong were no walkover, support for the war gradually diminished.

But in March 1968, a platoon of US soldiers on patrol entered into a hamlet in the jungle at a place called My Lai. There they executed about 500 villagers, the children, the elderly, and women. One Officer, Lieutenant William Calley, himself gunned-down 109 Vietnam citizens. Other soldiers added to the carnage on a large scale. At the time, the platoon were not under enemy fire.

The US Army suppressed information on all of this for 20 months, until two reporters broke the story, with photographic evidence. Calley was court marshalled in November, 1969, and found guilty on March 31, 1971. He was sentenced to life imprisonment with hard labour.

Over the next five years, legal and political battles shook the nation, as one legal institution after another decided either to free him or to incarcerate him. At one time, President Nixon demanded that Calley serve home-detention time rather than prison time. Gradually Calley's term of imprisonment was reduced, and he was finally released in September 1976.

Comments. The US was racked by dissension over the entire period. It came as a shock to most people that US troops could behave in this manner. As more and more reports of similar massacres emerged, ordinary people watching their evening meals were treated to photographic evidence that their own troops were committing War Crimes. Every one of many reports saw a drop in support for the war.

The same was **not** true for the public opinion of William Calley. Right through his trial, and the various moves to release and imprison him, up till his release, about 80 per cent of the population wanted him released. Some of this support came from those who thought Vietnamese "got what they deserved". Others felt that the US military did what they had to do, and that it was too easy to sit at a distance and judge them.

Many were imbued irrevocably with the certain knowledge that Communism was not just evil, but monstrous, and that the Reds were constantly repressing their citizens and imprisoning their captives and citizens at will. Nothing could shake this belief, and these Vietnamese, young and old, were part of the Evil Empire.

One US correspondent wrote:

Joseph Allsop, Washington. The persons Lt Calley was convicted of killing have been miscalled civilians. Above the level of really tiny children, they were no more civilians than was Lt Calley, although they did not wear uniforms.

The victims from My Lai in fact came from a "combat hamlet" of a "combat village." From about the age of four all persons in a VC "combat village," of both sexes, are trained to kill. By the iron rules of the Vietcong, if they do not follow their training they are killed themselves after one of the VC kangaroo trials.

On the other hand, others thought that Calley was just a scapegoat, and that the hatred that the Army taught their soldiers, and the contempt for human life, was the cause. So that many people higher up in the Army, and the nation, were the ones who should be on trial.

VIEWS ON CALLEY - FROM THE US

A correspondent to the *SMH*, working in the US, reported:

The public outcry against the conviction of William Calley, who admitted killing unarmed villagers in South Vietnam, is unprecedented in American history.

It is not a case of a few incurable militarists sending angry telegrams to the President. Tens of thousands of Americans, both in public and private life, have been moved to pick up their telephones or write or wire in protest.

Why?

Calley was convicted of the murders after a long and exhaustive court-martial by fellow American officers.

One of the jurors said the panel had tried to find some way of releasing Calley, but the young lieutenant had admitted the massacre on the witness stand. The jury had no alternative under law but to return the guilty verdict.

The public uproar that followed - and led to President Nixon's order to keep Calley out of prison during the long round of appeals - has produced hysterical and unreasoned cries.

But the most dominant theme is that it is unjust to convict Calley alone while others guilty of greater and lesser slaughter in Vietnam remain free and untried.

Many of the protestors are saying, in effect, that "we are all guilty." There is a growing clamour for a full-scale congressional inquiry into American "war crimes" in Vietnam, and yesterday seven Vietnam veterans were trying to surrender themselves as perpetrators. Christopher Vineyard said that as a forward air controller he directed bombings on many civilians.

Vietnam has brought home to millions of Americans - literally, through the TV screen - that indiscriminate killing in war is unavoidable, that war is a dirty business. These Americans, as they express it in private conversation, say Calley cannot be made to pay for the whole Vietnam tragedy.

The significance of the Calley protests goes this deeply for America. Most citizens want out of Vietnam, and no part of another foreign war - not in the Middle East or Pakistan or anywhere else.

A second Correspondent, also in America, raised other interesting points. He pointed out that at the end of WWII, at the US-led war-crimes trails, the Japanese General Yamashito was convicted and hanged because of atrocities that his troops had committed. Even though he had no knowledge of their actions, and would not have approved of them, it was found that the killings were part of his responsibility, and that he was guilty.

The Correspondent wrote that if Yamashito was guilty, then so too are the Generals who controlled Calley. "Or do we cynically admit that there is one law for the victor, and one for the vanquished. We should face the fact that the Yamashito case was simply an exercise in vengeance, rather law, and that it created a bad precedent.

"We must ask the question is it criminal to shoot unarmed prisoners on the ground, but legal to bomb them from the skies." "The soldier, be he friend or foe, is charged with the protection of the weak and unarmed. When he violates this sacred trust, he not only violates this trust, but threatens the very fabric of international society."

Comment. Strong words that reflect the passions aroused.

An Australian writer looked from a different point of view.

Letters, K Gee. Mr Suchting is right about genocide in South Vietnam, but wrong about the source from which it comes.

The killing of 100 men, women and children and the wounding of 96 others in the village of Duc Duc only a fortnight ago by a Vietcong "punishment squad" is but one example of the campaign of terror waged by the Communists against their own countrymen since Hanoi began its attempt to take over South Vietnam by force.

When I was in South Vietnam last August, the Government was delighted because the assassination rate had fallen to 200 a month, from 500 a month in earlier years. A week before my visit to the city of Hue, 25 people had been killed by a Russian rocket which landed in the market place. At the end of August, a raid by regular North Vietnamese Army men on a Buddhist orphanage at An Hoa had killed 15 children. In the year 1968 alone, the year of the Tet offensive, over 40,000 non-combatants were killed by Communist action.

Colonel Le Xuan Chuey, Chief of Staff of the 5th North Vietnamese Division, who defected in 1969, says that three million people are on the Communist lists for death or imprisonment. This may seem an exaggeration, until one relates the number of anti-Communists killed during the Communists' three-week occupation of Hue to the total population of South Vietnam.

This massive killing does not come from a criminal breach of military law by exhausted soldiers, as at My Lai, but from the use of terror as a primary weapon in the Communist arsenal for the breaking of an existing society and the substitution of the rule of the party elite.

We may be sure that nobody will go on trial for this genocide in Hanoi.

REACTION IN AUSTRALIA

Australia was different from America. We were not keen on Communists but we weren't paranoid about them. We were not all gung-ho about our Army, though we loved it when we had just wars. But was this a just war? Most of the population thought it was a disaster and foolish. Were we frightened about the Reds conquering all of Asia and Australia? Not at all.

But Calley did not disappear from the headlines in the US.

As he went before various Courts and Tribunals he always made headlines. In fact, he became something of a folk hero, and commanded much personal support. But, incidents of the killing of villagers was heard loud and clear in this nation, and this just about ended most support for the American war in Vietnam.

GETTING OUT OF VIETNAM

There is no doubt about it. The Yanks are getting tired of Vietnam. President Nixon announced that he will be reducing the number of troops by another 100,000 in second half of the year.

At its peak, the US had 549,000 troops there. After the next reduction, the level will be down to 184,000.

CHINA COMING OUT OF THE DOG HOUSE?

For the past 20 years, the US has refused to trade with China. This was despite the fact that there are huge trading opportunities available, especially in grain. But despite the lure of easy dollars, the US's ideological position was still firmly set against the Chinese.

President Nixon has suddenly lifted restraints in four small but symbolic areas. This may be the first sign that a thawing in the US-China relations could be on the cards.

If this developed into substantial trading between the two nations, it will be a great worry for our farmers in Australia.

TOM UREN RELEASED

Tom Uren was a well known Labor figure who was far to the Left, and who felt and acted vigorously against the Vietnam conscription and our presence there.

In September last year, he had joined a demonstration against the war, and had been arrested. He took a police officer to Court, claiming that he was man-handled. The charge was dismissed, and Uren was landed with $80 in costs. He was given about three months to pay, and this period ended in early April. He refused to pay, and was sentenced to three months hard labour.

After serving just 40 hours, he was released, because another Labor figure, Clive Evatt Junior, paid his fine. Uren was quite angry that he had been released as he had looked forward to be a martyr for the Cause.

He said that he was not anti-police, but against some police and the system that supported them.

Comment. This small report should remind you that the anti-war demonstrations were still going on.

SELLING OUT DOBELL

Letters, G Watt. I was indeed interested to glean details of a proposal to auction some 200 works by Sir William Dobell in order to augment the funds of the Dobell Foundation.

Indubitably, auctioneering firms will vie for the rights because the potential value of the works

- now classified as "virtually unknown" - is inestimable and therefore the trustees of the foundation would place an appropriate value on each, when framed and catalogued.

What does concern me, however, is that the auction method of realisation will probably result in the acquisition by other countries of works of art Sir William desired should not only benefit but, I feel sure, remain in this land.

The proceeds of auction presumably will be applied in full or invested for income purposes to further the promotion of art in Australia, as laid down in the terms of the bequest.

May I suggest that an alternative scheme be investigated? - namely, the retention of these 200 works by the trustees, and their annual hire to the many organisations, institutions and other bodies which attract public patronage and attendances, at an assessed fee. If so desired, a rotating exchange could be innovated.

Such an arrangement envisages - and desirably so - world coverage. Essentially, however, the works of Sir William would remain Australian-owned, and with the years enhancement of their value would accrue to Australia in conformity with what I feel sure was the desire of their donor.

CAN ANIMALS SEE COLOUR.

I know you have been waiting as patiently as you can for this question to be answered. So it is with much pleasure that I announce that the answer is now here.

Letters, John Henney. "We know that almost all the mammals, with the notable exceptions of the apes and monkeys, do not see colours at all." What is the evidence for this amazing statement, and who is "we"?

The mammals - dogs, cats, buffaloes, rhinoceroses, elephants and horses - have eyes structured the same way as man's. These animals possess the same rods and cones in the eyes, the same optic nerve, the same efferent and afferent nerves, and it is in the same part of the brain where the sensation of perception is somehow changed in to the picture of what we imagine we are seeing out there.

There is no evidence to lead us to believe that what another mammal sees is different in colour from what a man sees. It might well be that what Mr Gaston sees as blue his cat might see as red, but to claim that the cat cannot sense colour is taking too great a liberty with probability.

Mr Gunston's article is interesting and informative, but it might be a good idea if he gave the matter whether colour, as our eyes disclose it to be, is really there at all in physical space.

We see what we see because our eyes are what they are, and man's eyes closely resemble the eyes of the other mammals.

Comment. At last. Some clarity.

MAY NEWS ITEMS

Saturday. Anti-Vietnam protests were held in **Sydney**, with 2,000 people present. In **Adelaide** with 2,000. In **Brisbane**, with 5,000. In **Canberra**, with 3,000. In **Auckland**, with 10,000. There was no violence, and no arrests....

In **Washington**, large crowds gathered, and 200 protestors were arrested.

Aborigines in Northern Territory and Queensland were trying to get **some of the revenue that mining companies** were extracting from their traditional lands. A recent decision by the High Court meant that **they did not have formal ownership of the land** in many areas, including the Gove Peninsula....

A delegation arrived in Canberra with the intention of **pressing for a guaranteed minimum payment** of $250,000 a year from the mining companies. They were well received by the Prime Minister and Cabinet....

This was **one of the earliest steps in the saga** that later gave Aborigines extensive Land Rights in the nation.

Papua is under Australian administration. A magistrate there was confronted with **a boy who was found guilty of four charges** of breaking and entering. He was jailed for six months on each of the four charges....

This might seem to be consistent with the Australian concept of justice. However, it has caused some consternation because **the child is only 9 years of age**. He will be **in prison with adult male offenders**....

The magistrate regretted the matter, and said he was aware that the child would be badly influenced by adult criminals. but said he had no alternative because **the Territory has no reformatory suitable for minors**.

In 1949, Mao Tse Tung ended his Long March and his battles against the Chinese Nationalist Government, and was able to declare victory. **China was now a Communist nation.** The USA and Britain and other western nations, including Australia, immediately stated that they would **not recognise the new Government**, and would cut all trade and ties....

Australia, over the years, has relaxed this attitude to **allow trade between the two countries**. But we still officially do not recognise them, we vote to exclude them from the UN, and we keep up a constant stream of propaganda that all things Red, including China, are terribly bad....

America is showing **some signs of relenting**. We are too. **Prime Minister** McMahon announced that we will be **seeking "dialogue"** through diplomatic channels with the Chinese. Our Opposition Leader, **Gough Whitlam, has gone one further** and said that he, and three other Shadow Ministers, will go to China, and talk with Government and a host of others, **to open up another "dialogue"**....

This is a big turnround in policy. Maybe the anti-Chinese propaganda will ease up a bit, and allow some truth to come through. Maybe we can drop our travel ban and travel there and see for ourselves.

DO YOU REMEMBER....?
A few Letters filled me with nostalgia.

Wine flagons. Remember those large bottles made of glass, that came into view at barbies and late on Saturday nights at dinner parties? They held about three bottles, and never pretended to be anything but plonk. They were popular because they were cheap, and they were always there when the good stuff ran out.

Of course, they have gone now. They have been replaced by casks, with their plastic innards and cute little taps. The good thing is that the quality of the wine therein has remained as it always was, and the hangover is still a reminder of old times.

One writer reminded me of these flagons when he talked about the problem of getting rid of the empties. The suppliers will not take them back, and he says that a policy of "disposal by dispersal" applies. That in fact, "we just chuck them anywhere we can".

He argues that industry should find new ways of recycling flaggons and bottles generally. In later years, and indeed in previous years, paying refunds on some bottles became popular, as did the idea of putting bottles into separate garbage bins.

He highlights a problem that persists and we as a society keep scratching the surface of. That is, if flagons have gone, and other things have changed, what do we do with the packaging? In 2020 terms, what do we do with the plastic involved?

Solutions come and go, but the problem remains.

Milk bottles. Another writer reminded me of milk bottles. He regrets their passing. He talked about the earlier years when milk was home-delivered, and the jug with a little cotton cover was placed over it. Then came the same milko but now with full bottles for the milk, and the half bottles for cream.

He liked those bottles. And he points out that they did not pile up and become a nuisance, because once a week the milko came later in the day and collected them.

"It's a sad day when you can't walk out onto your verandah and get your milk. No one wants to walk two miles to get fresh milk. If this is progress, you can keep it,"

Theatre organs. In the 1920's, goers had only silent films to watch. So in the major cites of the world, including Australia, large city theatres introduced pipe organs to enhance moments of drama with appropriate bursts of deep throbbing music. By the 1930's, and then during the War, there was plenty of sound coming from the movies themselves, but the pipe-organs lingered on.

By then, they greeted patrons with classical or serious music as they entered and waited for the first movie, then started up again at half-time, and at the end.

By about 1950, the pipe-organs were generally on their way out. The grand instruments, just beside the stage, had about twenty pipes rising vertically into the air. Each pipe was from 10 to 20 feet high, and in front sat a maestro in full evening dress pumping out the chords.

Alas, **by 1971**, all of these had disappeared from theatres.

But at least one writer remembered them. He points out that several of them have found new homes in Town Halls, and they have even been installed in private homes. And, he says, electronic imitations have appeared on the scene. These latter have the advantages of being cheaper and of a convenient size.

But, no, they do not compare. He yearns for the characteristic grandeur and original splendour of the full-sized pipe-organs.

Comment. As a county-born child, when we visited The Big City at Christmas once a year, we would go to the theatre half an hour early to listen to the pipe-organ. I miss this. Just as I miss the Peters ice cream and lollies from the lads and lasses with trays moving up and down the aisles.

IT'S ALL BLACK AND WHITE
The battle between blacks and whites in South Africa is getting closer to our shores. As we have seen, the whites there have most of the power, property and wealth. The blacks, although forming a vast majority, have very little of these. Without attempting at all to describe this situation, it is fair to say that at the moment the blacks are trying to change this in their favour, and the whites are fighting to retain their privileged position.

As part of this, the whites have developed a policy called **Apartheid** that keeps the blacks separate from the whites in all walks of life, and have enacted laws to enforce this.

In Australia, disputes over this policy have been festering for months. Is it justified because it is the whites whose hard work and capital have made the nation what it is today? Or should not the blacks have control over their own land and resources and wealth, and the very lives of their population?

We have been arguing for quite a while about whether we should welcome the upcoming **cricket** tour by the South Africans. But this is still months away. Right now, the issue has suddenly hit the headlines **because it has been decided that a South African Rugby Union tour, with no black players, will come to Australia next month.**

Below is a sample of the wide-ranging debate on the proposed visit.

> **Letters, G Charles.** It would be difficult to find bigger hypocrites than those correspondents who write in your columns attacking the visits of South African teams to Australia.
>
> There is no excuse for any lack of knowledge of the appalling conditions in which **native Australians** are expected to exist today. Regularly the *ABC* (to its credit) presents documentaries showing the situation in detail **in different parts of Australia**. Recently we have seen this in Cunnamulla, Wyndham, the Queensland coastal concentration camps, Glen Innes, and many other places.

Mr Charles follows this with four paragraphs where he points out many areas where our own Aborigines are badly dealt with. He singles out the "pass" laws in many States that restrict free movement to and from Reserves. And the many cases where they get less than justice before the Law. And the exploitation of Aborigines in the labour market.

And in the appalling incidence of death and disease among their people. **He continues on.**

If these vociferous anti-South African agitators devoted even a fraction of their time and energy to improving the lot of Australian Aborigines, they might be considered less dishonest. As it stands they are exploiting the ignorance and apathy of the Australian public in relation to Australia's own colour problem, for purely selfish political gains.

Letters, R Cullinane. The Rev Alan Walker is reported to have distinguished between the South African cricket tour and the present tour of the Moscow Circus on the ground that as far as he knew Moscow Circus members were not chosen on the basis of race or colour.

Has he thought it necessary to inquire whether any performers were excluded from the circus tour **because they were not ideologically "clean"**?

It seems that as far as Mr Walker is concerned it is right and necessary to protest against the denial of individual rights to people who happen to be black, but not right and necessary to protest against the denial of individual rights to people who happen to be white.

Is this not racism?

Letters, J Nelson and S Bell. The demonstrations and union bans being planned for the South African sporting team's visit to Australia are completely unreasonable.

What right have Australians to dictate who should represent South Africa in any team it should select? Australians are very quick to tell the rest of the world that it has no right interfering with their immigration policies, so why should this minority group try to force its ideas on the selectors of South African teams?

Letters, J Hootman. There seems to be a reasonable formula under which the tour can still take place without loss of principle, to either point of view, and which may be readily acceptable to the respective officials.

This is that an all-white side be called "a South African XI," which no one can surely dispute. And the matches be not regarded as official international Tests.

Letters, J Thornett, Capt Australian Rugby Team in South Africa 1963. Also toured South Africa in 1961, 1964. I believe the Australian Rugby Football Union reflects the wishes of the vast majority of Australians in its decision to proceed with the tour by the South Africans.

I am sure that few, if any, Australians condone the concept of Apartheid either morally or practically, but I wonder how many of the protesters would dissent so vigorously if they had been brought up in those extremely difficult conditions. Not one in a hundred, I would suggest.

Our own record on racial understanding, has been appalling. **Our restrictive immigration policies are notorious.** It is sheer hypocrisy for us to attempt to interfere in another country's internal racial policies, especially when that country's problems so far outweigh our own.

If current attempts to stop sporting contests continue, it is quite possible that Australia will be the next target of similar anti-racial protest. Who, of our people, would enjoy the prospect of our sporting teams being refused access to another country because of our Government policies, racial or otherwise? Why should our Asian neighbours not use this technique to influence a change in our immigration laws, or even our trading policies?

It is tragic that sport, this wonderful medium of human relations, which has hitherto been devoid of political interference, can be so threatened.

No government policy in the world receives more constant and more adverse publicity than Apartheid. It is hard to imagine any country being as intolerable as the publicity would have it. Certainly, one sees in South Africa examples of racial prejudice degrading to the unfortunate non-white people, but little evidence of widespread unhappiness or poverty among them.

Yes, we may all hold strong anti-Apartheid views; but let us get our own house in order before shouting so loud. Above all, let us keep Australian sport independent of political interests. **Let us play, without prejudice, anyone willing to play us, so that both sides gain understanding from the experience.**

Comment. Thornett's sober thoughts do seem to echo what ordinary Australians thought.

But what if the tour actually eventuates. What will be the opinion of Joe Blow then?

A POST SCRIPT LETTER ON CALLEY

Letters, P Flanagan. There is **no justification whatsoever for J Alsop's claim** that Lieutenant Calley's crime at My Lai consisted in the killing of enemy combatants and their allies

1."Newsweek," not noted for left-wing bias, correctly described the matter: "The offense of which Lieutenant Calley was found guilty was rounding up defenseless inhabitants - men, women, children, and babies - of a village from which his troops reported receiving no hostile fire and killing them in cold blood."

2. You endorse editorially Mr Alsop's view that My Lai was an isolated aberration, as follows: "The Vietnam war is not like My Lai. No evidence, except My Lai, has been unearthed to show that US military policy ever demanded any such indiscriminate slaughter."

On the contrary, the evidence is overwhelming. See, for example, Edward Herman's "Atrocities in Vietnam: Myths and Realities," Chomsky's "At War with Asia," "The Indochina Story" by the Concerned Asian Scholars.

My Lai is merely the most publicised of American war crimes. Far more important has been the **systematically indiscriminate air destruction of the peoples of Indo-China**.

That such systematic destruction of the civilian population constitutes a massive war crime under the Nuremberg principles of 1950 is beyond dispute. A recent "New York Times" book review **discusses 33 books on the question of American war crimes. Both you (the *SMH*) and Mr Alsop contrive to ignore these facts**.

Comment. Without wishing to lay the boot into our American friends, it seems that they have often in the past, and will also in the future, contrived to ignore unpleasant facts. But are Australians also guilty of this? My considered opinion is that they have been, and will be in future. The **extent** to which they do so is perhaps a point of difference with the Americans.

SMOKE GETS IN YOUR EYES

The Letter below reflects the common perception about smoking. It regretted the proliferation of advertising, compares its evils to those of alcohol, and calls for education on the matter.

Letters, Andrew Burns. This habit, a dirty habit, survives only because of advertisements that show handsome people lounging about having a smoke. If you took away those lizards the whole tobacco industry would collapse. It is the same as drinking alcohol. The glamour sells tobacco,

We need education in our youngsters before it is too late. There is no way you can change the mobs drinking in pubs. You have to get the children and teens, while they are young. Turn the tables on the advertisers, and get them while they are still young.

Yet, there was large and growing evidence that smoking was a killer through lung cancer and other diseases. This information was not hidden, it was not tucked away in some obscure medical journal. It was in plain sight, barking at smokers and Authorities, there for all to see.

Overseas, especially in Britain, the general public was **showing limited signs** of recognising the links between smoking and cancer. **Here, however, the change in attitude was not at all evident.** See, for example, the above Letter that does not give the link even a mention.

Of course, the above writer is partially right. Advertising played a vital role in supporting the market. But so too was the reluctance of the typical smoker to give up a habit that had no immediate bad consequences. "Old Bill smoked all his life, and lived to 200." The idea of not smoking was just something that could not be contemplated, it meant a whole change in lifestyle and comfort levels.

It has taken 50 years to slowly change the mind of half, or more, of the population. And yet, **even now,** in the 2020's, smokers can be seen congregating in bays outside buildings, pursuing their wilful ways.

Comment. I do not think that these smokers are ignorant of the dangers. A few might deny them and they are all prepared to take the risk. It's the same type of risk we all take when we get into a car. **And for them, smoking is worth the risk.** And, in any case, remember Old Bill.

JUNE NEWS ITEMS

Audie Murphy, a hero from WWII and a noted Hollywood actor, **died in a private plane crash.**

Last Thursday, a man phoned Police and said he had placed **a bomb on a jet leaving Sydney** for Hong Kong, and **it would explode soon**. Convinced that this was a genuine threat, **Qantas made a payment of $500,000 to the man**, **called Mr Brown**. The plane turned back to Sydney....

After the payment, Brown rang police and **said there was no bomb on board**. Over the last few days, Police have been flooded with similar calls, and all of them have been hoaxes....

Today, Police acknowledged that **they have as yet no leads** on who the culprit might be.

In 1969, the Federal Government **agreed to build a power-generating nuclear power plant** at Jervis Bay, on the south east coast of this nation. It was **initially planned to open in 1977**. The largest near-by city was Canberra....

Now **the construction has been delayed for a year**, due mainly to cost blow-outs. And, of course, a change in political leadership of the Government....

The plant was never built. Australia has no nuclear power plants.

William McBride was a physician operating out of Sydney's prestigious Crown Street Hospital. In 1971, he was awarded   several world-class honours for his work on pointing out that the drug **thalidomide caused multiple defects in babies**. ...

Using the prize money he established a research foundation and by 1981 was advocating the use of the drug Debendox to help pregnant mothers. But in 1993, **he was struck off the medical register** for falsifying research results relating to the drug....

He was restored to the register in 1998. It was said that his deceptive work was **a major cause of uncertainty for pregnant women** and their carers for a dozen years.

A Sydney boy had **his upper arm badly damaged** by a large **fire cracker**. He developed an ailment called gas gangrene, an extremely virulent organism which thrives on tissues deprived of oxygen....

He is now in hospital in emergency care, in a hyperbaric chamber, and is **"holding his own"**....

Two 10-year-olds are also in hospital, each hoping to preserve their sight **after cracker accidents.** This of course, is a consequence of **fireworks bonfires during the Queen's Birthday celebrations**.

A police constable gave evidence to a Tweed Heads magistrate that a man looked at him and **made an "Oink, Oink, Oink" noise**. The man was fined $60. The SM, in commenting, said that it was apparent that the **word "pig" was often used in Sydney** as a description of police. He hoped that **such usage would never spread** to other parts of Australia.

COMPULSORY SEAT BELTS

The NSW Government has decided that seat belts in cars must be worn by drivers and passengers, starting probably from August 1st. A variety of regulations have been published that allow for age and type of vehicle, and many exemptions have been made.

For example, people over 70 years of age will be excused. So too will drivers of home delivery vehicles travelling at under 15 miles per hour. There is no decision yet on interstate drivers, nor on those from Canberra. Some cars will need front and back seat fittings, and others will need only front fittings. There are heaps of matters that will need sorting out, but the intention is clear. That is, the wearing of seat belts will become compulsory from August 1st.

For a couple of years prior to this, the use of seat belts has been voluntary, and new cars generally have been fitted with them. But now, fines of $20 will apply to **passengers**, and drivers. The owners of cars that are not fitted properly will be liable for a fine of $40.

The idea behind these regulations is to save lives and prevent injuries in the event of a collision. Obviously, this is a good cause. But there were objections.

Letters, K Powell. The decision of the NSW Government to defer legislation making the wearing of seat belts compulsory encourages me to urge that this type of legislation be dropped entirely from the Government's legislative program.

I realise that my suggestion will be unpopular with many people, and let me add that I, personally, wear a seat belt, and I think that people who don't are acting foolishly. Moreover, I applaud legislation to make the fitting of seat belts compulsory.

But whether the individual takes advantage of this or not **is for him to decide**. Failure to do so endangers no one else but himself. It is a gross erosion of individual freedom when, for this type of offence, a policeman can impose an on-the-spot fine, which is what it would amount to. Moreover, it is unfair to the police force, who are already loaded down with the enforcement of laws which have nothing to do with crime prevention, and which add to their unpopularity.

My critics will point to the cost of accidents to the community. This is a red herring. If this type of thinking were carried to a logical conclusion, we would have the type of society that exists in Russia or China. Those who are unconcerned about the progressive erosion of individual liberty can always find strong arguments for compulsion in many fields.

Those who would support seat-belt legislation of the kind suggested may care to think about the health costs to the community of alcohol, sedatives, aspirin, cigarettes and a whole range of human indulgences.

Letters, W Lovell. I hope Mr Morris will consider very carefully before legislating for the compulsory use of seat belts.

Has anyone considered the possibility that **the increase in accidents in recent years may be linked to the increasing use of seat belts**, in that they have a bad psychological effect on some drivers, inducing a false sense of security? This could account for the increasing display of arrogance and lack of courtesy by many drivers.

Furthermore, as it is impossible to fully police existing traffic regulations, what possible chance is there of policing the use of seat belts? I feel it will merely be relegated to the same status as certain other regulations, such as speed limits, and used solely for the purpose of collecting revenue.

The majority of accidents are caused by rank bad driving and anti-social behaviour and it would appear that no Government has the moral courage to implement the only remedy. This involves ensuring that traffic police are non-identifiable, whether in cars or on motor cycles, and that the law is administered with justice and commonsense and not used merely to raise revenue.

There were many others who thought differently.

Letters, R Simpson. It is mere sophistry to argue, as does K Powell, that the compulsory wearing of seat belts constitutes "progressive erosion of individual liberty." But with even less logic, Mr Powell goes on to dismiss the communal cost of road accidents as "a red herring."

To follow this line of thought to its logical conclusion, we should permit the individual to indulge in a variety of other anti-social activities - from drug-taking to indecent exposure - all in the name of individual liberty.

This confusion of licence with liberty is something which I, as a member of the Council for Civil Liberties, emphatically reject.

The plain facts are that road accidents fill more of our (subsidised) hospital beds than any other cause; that many are injured for every one killed on the roads; that of the injured many are young people who, through brain damage, will remain dependent upon the community for the rest of their lives. This is no "red herring"; it is the real tragedy of the road toll; it is a community cost in wasted lives that we cannot continue to ignore.

One wonders how many of the living victims would agree with Mr Powell?

Personal Comment. Those who argue for civil liberties are important as watchdogs over governmental and corporate abuses. **It does not matter that in many cases, their warnings wear thin with the passage of time.** For example, the opposition to seat belts, and the arguments against drunk driving have given way to the common appreciation of their efficacy.

In fact, their arguments **do often** put a brake on some schemes that would not turn out to be winners. So then their efforts are of value.

Yet, those who argue for civil liberties should remember that **with liberties also come responsibilities, and respect for consequences, and such things as concern for law and order**.

My contention is that civil liberty is **just one piece** of a parcel that we all inherit. **To use that liberty alone as a defense to deny all community progress hardly seems justified.**

ENVIRONMENTALISTS ON THE MARCH

They're everywhere! They're everywhere! People all over the nation found that their environment was being threatened by all sorts of changes, and were clubbing together and screaming for rectification. They were starting now to think of acting as **political p**arties, and in Tasmania were organising to run candidates in next year's State elections. By doing this, they would become the first Green Party in the world to do this.

What were their problems? It's hard to know where to start, but a few obvious ones come to mind. For example, the atmosphere was full of smoke, the airlines were polluting our noise corridors, land developers were gobbling up our bushland, roads were being cut through pasture, animals were being kept in cages, bowling clubs were invading public parks, and waves were washing away our foreshores and beaches.

I could go on. You are, in the 2020's, very familiar with them all, but in early 1970's, these disclosures fell on innocent ears and gained recruits for movements that grew to the extent that, a decade later, the Green Party was able to run a host of candidates in the **Federal** elections.

In passing, let me give you a mixed-bag of protests.

Letters, R Taylor. It seems that the Government's whitewash brush has been handed on to the air pollution control branch of the Department of Public Health.

I have no idea what status the "spokesman" has in the department, but his suggestion that Tuesday's smog could have been caused by a dust storm or some other natural phenomenon is absolutely ludicrous.

The Weather Bureau's explanation of the cause is simple and logical. The bureau blames smoke from factories, cars and power stations, trapped under a layer of cloud, with no wind to disperse it. Of course this is not the first time that this set of circumstances has occurred, and unfortunately it will not be the last.

I live on a hill overlooking the Harbour, with a wide view to the Blue Mountains. All too often the view vanishes.

There certainly was a component of dust in Tuesday's atmosphere, some of it from Sydney's worst source of pollution, Pyrmont power station, which is the main cause of the inner City haze whenever the air is still and damp. Regardless of the cost, Pyrmont station should have been closed long ago - and would have been by any Government which had any real regard for public health.

BITS OF OLD BUSH

Earlier this week the "Herald" published a letter satirically hailing the victory of development over conservation at Kelly's Bush - the 6 acres of natural bushland at Hunters Hill which the Minister for Local Government has gazetted as a site for 25 houses: "We'll have the bulldozers in no time. Then the builders. Then the real estate boys. We'll all make a jolly good profit out of that bit of old bush."

Many in Sydney, who have any feeling against the steady despoliation of its bushland, will share the writer's anger.

The Editor went on to detail a how a Council in Sydney gave permission to denude trees and bushland for the building of tennis courts. Another Council surrendered five acres for a bowling Club. A third Council has donated land for the construction of a 40-acre public park. He went on with other examples.

He then concludes:

> Groups of citizens are, indeed, fighting most of these moves. They need all the support and assistance they can get, for recent history suggests that they do not often win. Does the sporting life really breed healthy minds in healthy bodies? Apparently not any more - only the arrogant selfishness that says let the rest of the public go hang.

> **Letters, M Newlinds.** An aerodrome at Duffys Forest is being pressed again. We are told that a sum of $500,000 is to be spent.

The protest committee naturally has the support of local residents and various amateur conservation groups, none of whom is wealthy or powerful.

The proponents of the aerodrome are backed by powerful commercial and Government interests.

My main point is the disappointment we feel in the National Parks and Wildlife Service. This is the Government Department which administers Ku-ring-gai Chase, on whose border the aerodrome is to be built, and which agreed to the transfer of some of its parkland to the aerodrome.

The same Government Department has a policy to repurchase freehold property at Cottage Point and on the west side of Pittwater with public money. I presume that this is to preserve tranquility and minimise habitation on these borders.

How can the same Government Department be so lukewarm in its opposition to an aerodrome and even go to the extent of handing over land to it on the southern boundary of the same national park? Are double standards such as these legitimate?

Comment.   Over the course of months, the number of such Letters was growing quickly. Some of them were deadly serious, like losing forests to mining. Others were of lesser real concern. But in all cases, the writers were **concerned** enough to write to the Editor. The Environment was changing from a fad to a serious issue, with thousands of people wakening to the threat now becoming publicly discussed.

BACK IN THE PARTY

Jack Lang was one of the most remarkable politicians that this nation has seen. He was born in 1876, and lived his childhood, and indeed, his life, close to poverty. He entered politics when he was elected as Lord Mayor of Sydney's Auburn from 1909 to 1913, and as Treasurer for the State of NSW from 1920 to 1922, He was later elected as Leader of the Opposition in 1925, and then became Premier of the State after Labor's election win in 1925.

I can hear you thinking that this was a pretty good performance so far, but hardly "most remarkable." Well, let me agree with you, but let me also say that from there he upped the pace. Vide....

In his first term as Premier, he introduced a heap of Labor's many programmes. Such as workers' compensation for death or injury, and the abolition of fees for High Schools in State schools. He also started child endownment, and the 44-hour working week.

He allowed women to sit as Members in the Upper House, and he established universal suffrage in local elections. Previously the only people who could vote were property owners in a major city.

In 1930, he regained his job as Premier. The nation and the State were in the middle of the Depression. Unlike other political leaders world-wide, he refused to cut expenses and jobs, but that policy forced NSW into greater debt.

He decided, in 1930, that the way out was to "repudiate" this nation's debt to the British Government and bond holders in Britain. This was large, given the Sydney

Harbour Bridge had been financed by them. By repudiate, he meant to not pay interest on the debt, and as an offshoot, he also meant to control interest rates so that it paid only three per cent - way below the current rate - on all other debt.

This was a spectacular proposal, and put him at odds with the other States, and with the Commonwealth, and with the banks, both at home and abroad. He implemented the "Lang Plan" as best he could in NSW, amid scathing criticism from the other parties involved. This dissension spread to the Federal Parliament, and the Labour Government was thrown out.

But in NSW, the Labour Party was completely split into two factions by the disruption. **Lang was dismissed by the Governor,** and the Labor Party was well beaten in the ensuing election.

Lang continued to lead the Labor Party until 1939. He was expelled in 1942. He continued to seek public office for almost a decade after this, with many, many voters supporting his Lang Labour Party. In this period, he entered into **a dozen controversies** that continued to split the Labor Party.

He was re-admitted to the Labor Party in 1971. He died in 1975, aged 98.

NOTES ON LANG

Lang's first term. I encourage you to look back at his first term. **He led the world** on each of those matters, despite resistance from all corners of the globe. Imagine how different our world would have been if these advances had not been made.

Sir Phillip Game. Lang withdrew all State money from the Commonwealth Bank, and **held them in a mountain of cash in Trades Hall**. The Governor, Sir Phillip Game, told him that this was illegal. Lang would not reverse, so Game sacked him. It is reported by Lang himself, and by other reputable writers, that Lang gave serious consideration to arresting the Governor.

The sacking of Lang was the first time in the nation's history that a Vice-Regal person dismissed a Parliamentary Leader. The second time was when the Governor General sacked Prime Minister Gough Whitlam in 1975.

The opening of the Sydney Harbour Bridge in 1932 was the scene of a memorable occasion. There was a massive crowd there to witness, and all the governors, politicians, clergy, Press, and officials were packed into grandstands and the whole length of the Bridge. It was scheduled to be opened by Lang.

But a Major de Groot, of the paramilitary Home Guard, got there first on his horse, and cut it with a few slashes of his sword. The ribbon was rejoined, Lang cut it, and de Groot was later fined five Pounds for Offensive Behaviour.

My Uncle Bill now gets a mention among all these dignitaries. He was a life-long NSW Public Servant. He was very considered, deliberate, and knew how to keep himself to himself. Every year, he and his family visited us in the country for a couple of weeks. And we visited them in the city for a similar period.

In the evenings, we would gather round the wooden kitchen table, for the evening "tea". A delight to me over the years was when my father baited Bill about Lang Labour. Bill turned from "wouldn't hurt a fly" mode into an Adolf Hitler. He thought the Lang Plan was the only way to live, that Lang had been sent here from Heaven to remove the Pommy yoke, and that our public debt should never be repaid. "The buggers have milked us since the First Fleet".

After an hour of this, each night, the adults would usher him off to bed. Next morning he would emerge, and the flies were safe again.

Uncle Bill encapsulated the feelings that the common man held towards Lang. We were proud of our brief heritage as a nation, and were prepared to guard it jealously despite the fact that over half the population was of first- or second -generation British stock. The English Government and their ilk were fair game for exploitation in reverse.

So, over half the nation were happy with repudiation. Of course this would have been disastrous for the nation. But, forget logic, we don't need **their** money any more. So Lang was, to a million people, a hero, a populist saviour of a nation struggling with the Depression.

Further comment. To me, Lang's record is remarkable. I could say that only Gough Whitlam, with his vision, and the quieter but determined Bob Menzies, could stand in the same paddock.

I suppose I have to be sensible, **maybe my judgement has been warped by Uncle Bill**. But, then again, maybe not. **You be the judge.**

JULY NEWS ITEMS

Three Russian cosmonauts died as they returned to earth after 23 days in space. Ground controllers had no idea that anything was amiss until the recovery crew opened their re-entry capsule....

Theories abound as to what caused their deaths. Their mission had been successful up to this point.

Qantas **had** resolved to **ground all its hostesses at age 35.** They have now **postponed** the implementation of this.

A Swedish-born **New Zealander has landed in Madagascar after rowing for four months westwards for 4,400 miles across the Indian Ocean from Perth.**

The NSW Education Department will eliminate sports day from all schools. Previously one afternoon a week had been allocated for sport. The aim is to allow for other subjects, and new subjects, to be pursued.

It is expected that 25,000 people will be camping out **at Mount Turu in New Guinea next Wednesday.** This is because the Yangoru Cargo-cult has advised that at that spot **the cargo will appe**ar. They include white man's possessions such as planes, TVs and radios....

Christian missionaries there are concerned because of the apparent failure to displace primitive beliefs with their more sophisticated beliefs.

The University of NSW is offering to pay 50 cents each for about **100 blue-ringed octopuses. They should**

still be alive, or deepfrozen soon after capture. It is prepared to make home visits to collect the specimens that will be used for research into their deadly poison.

President Nixon, speaking at a conference of 135 news executives said "**the great civilisations of the past**, as they have become wealthy, and as they have lost their will to live, to improve, **have become subject to the decadence that eventually destroys the civilisation. America is now reaching that point."**

Comment. There was a lot of speculation about his intent. Was he really telling America to behave itself? Quite a few people thought that, being a Quaker, he would be inclined to warn the nation about decadence.

The Bee Gees are back in Australia. They left Australia in 1967, and split up in 1969. But they are back together as a group, and on their way to **a tour of New Zealand.** They would be happy to do the same in Australia. **That would be delight to their many fans here.**

The Minister for Health said that **dogs and cats from the UK will be allowed into this country in future.** The ban on this was introduced in 1969 after two incidents with two dogs that developed rabies....

But the new regulations are demanding **12 months in quarantine in the UK, six weeks on the High Seas, and two months in quarantine here.**

Gough Whitlam is back from China, saying he wants to **resume relations with that country.** The Government, on the other hand, is standing firmly against this.

THE ALL WHITE RUBGY TOUR

The South Africans Rugby team made it here. You will remember that the team is all white, despite the fact that there were some blacks who should have been in the team based on merit.

But that was not to be. So the team flew to Melbourne, and worked their way up and down the eastern States.

THE SCENE IN MELBOURNE

The newspaper heading was **POLICE CHARGE.**

The leading paragraphs said "Mounted police, batons flailing, charged anti-Apartheid demonstrators at the Springboks match today. There were scenes of unprecedented violence at Melbourne Park Oval.

> More than 600 police made mass arrests, during an afternoon of repeated bloody confrontation. Mounted police frequently charged the demonstrators, and police on foot flayed them with batons. Small groups of demonstrators who ran onto the ground were run down and trampled by police horses.

The reporter went on to describe how a protest meeting of about 6,000 persons was held in a down-town park. All fired up, they marched en masse to the Oval. There they were confronted by 600 police. They searched many demonstrators and found they were carrying dangerous weapons as well as big crackers. A crowd of about 5,000 was eventually let into the ground. On five occasions, some of these invaded the pitch during play.

The players took no notice of the off-field happenings. About 200 were formally arrested, and hundreds of others were chucked out of the ground.

Later that night, when the Springboks arrived at their Sydney hotel, they were greeted with verbal abuse by a crowd of about 300.   Matters were generally orderly, but later, 11 people were arrested for trying to enter the hotel. The organisers of the rally were delighted with the attendance, and the enthusiasm of the dissidents. They opined that surely now, the tour would be cancelled. **But they were wrong.**

LATER MATCHES
At the Sydney Cricket Ground's first match, organisers for the protesters guaranteed the Police that their protest would be orderly. There would be no violence, and no weapons.

But when the game came to the field, 2,000 of the 18,000 crowd, did demonstrate. They threw missiles such as cans and crackers, onto the field, and thousands of tacks designed to hobble horses. 600 police were there to control them, and a 10-foot-high 3-strand barbed wire fence helped in that. A few runners got onto the field, but were caught by police and put into vans.

In all, it was less violent than Melbourne. Only 55 were arrested. But it showed that opposition to the Tour was still strong.

At the second match at the SCG, with a crowd that was double that of the previous match, things were again lively, but the police were getting more and more experienced. Maybe the situation was easing.

But not necessarily so. The Queensland Government announced the **Order of a State of Emergency** for the Team's visit. Since the team was to be in the State for three weeks, there were suggestions that this was overkill. But Premier Bjelke-Petersen was a well-known law-and-order man, so the Order stayed.

Members of the powerful Queensland Trades and Labor Council declared a one-day strike against the Order.

So masses of police, with barbed wire and dogs, were ready for Saturday's match. But nothing happened. The Tourists came to the ground, played a match of footy, and went back to their hotel. No problems, no hooting, no crackers, no riots. Just like any other game of Saturday football. Bjelke-Petersen crowed.

From there on, the tour was not very eventful. The demonstrators claimed victory They were pleased with the huge numbers that they attracted, and they hoped that the South African cricket tour would be cancelled.

The Rugby Union and other Authorities claimed victory in that no games were stopped, and all were completed. They pointed out that the demonstrators were mostly university students, who traditionally liked a bit of rough stuff on their week-ends.

The tour lasted for six weeks from June 26th until August 7th. It had 13 matches on its agenda, and the ones that I did not report on were miniature versions of the ones that I did report.

Comment. Overall, the demonstrations had a lasting effect. Most other South African teams, like women's hockey, cancelled their projected tours, and for a decade or more, South Africa was often regarded as a pariah State. **But more of this later.**

THE CONCORDE

The French were currently busy designing and building a prototype of a very fast plane. It was expected to fly at a speed in excess of the speed of sound, and to go from London to New York in only a few hours. This plane was hailed as an engineering triumph, and it was said that it created the beginning of a new age for business travel.

The attention of the entire aviation world was focused on France, and every announcement from there was greeted with excitement and cheers.

But not every one agreed. This Letter below was from a scientist at the CSIRO, and he did his best to pour cold water on the development.

Letters, J Goldberg (principal research scientist, CSIRO). For human, social and scientific reasons, I take issue with those who assert that the supersonic transport is a fact of life, and a necessary step to progress. Progress for whom? And for what?

Consider now the first, or human, case. Take a hypothetical wealthy businessman, his fares paid by his company, his hormonal balance not too normal after years of stressful living, his total physical fitness in doubt after years of commuting in company cars, in overcrowded cities, and also because of over-eating and drinking at business luncheons.

Our man takes his seat in a supersonic jet, his briefcase bulging with important, stress-producing documents. He is going abroad at high speed to clinch some deal which will produce greater profits. He has been overfed with airline food and liquor and stimulated by attention from pretty airline hostesses.

Here is a human being well set-up for a heart attack, subjected to further disturbances to the natural circadian rhythm of the body by an upset in hormonal balance and correlated effects due to time-zone changes.

In the meantime, before he collapsed, he will be tormented by the excessive noise that the craft emits. This noise actually wrecks building as the plane flies overhead in flight, and breaks mirrors as it takes off.

Is this really progress? I call it torture.

Letters, Luchen Boz, Public Relations Officer for the French Aerospace Manufacturers. Mr J Goldberg uses many well-worm criticisms of the Concorde SST.

Aerospatiale, the company responsible for the French share of the Concorde program, in co-operation with BAC, has produced figures in answer to the charge of pollution of the environment.

As far as the sonic boom is concerned, at a press conference in Sydney on April 14, 1970, Mr Jacques Noetinger, chief of the press service of the French Aerospace Manufacturers, said that "noise problems at Mascot as well as the other international airports would be solved in the near future" and that within five years new international regulations would come into effect to reduce the present level of noise.

Benefiting from the experience acquired with the two Franco-British prototypes, noise levels have been reduced on the Olympus jet engine which will power the three preproduction Concordes and the production units.

Comment. Despite the cold water, and the cost overruns, and the long delays, the Concorde eventually began commercial travel in 1976. It continued to fly until it was terminated in 2003. Its cross-Atlantic travel speed was half that of its nearest competitor, and it appealed to the relatively few wealthy that could afford the high price that was demanded.

The Governments of Britain and France financed the building of the plane. And they supported it through a long period of losses. But the plane could only fly over oceans, because of the sonic boom. Eventually, losses got too big, the sponsors pulled the plug, and the supersonic flights across the Atlantic ceased.

Letters, W Adams. Being unable to obtain woollen blankets 108in x 117in in Australia, I wrote to the United States and found that blankets were obtainable in that size, but made of acrylic and nylon vellux. No woollen blankets were available at all!

No further evidence need be shown to deduce that wool as the world's fibre is finished.

The woolgrower is not alone in the position he is now in; it happened in five short years to the Japanese silkworm grower and to the Brazilian and Malaysian rubber producers.

The growers must accept this.

SPORT IN SCHOOLS

The decision to remove compulsory sport from the Curriculum raised a lot of eyebrows. The Education Department says that this is necessary to alleviate a shortage of teachers. It has tried to overcome this by recruiting overseas, especially in Canada.

Another way out of the shortage is to give up an afternoon of sport once a week and thereby free up teachers to actually teach. People had differing ideas on the subject.

The *SMH* liked it. It pointed out that the savings would be the equivalent of adding 700 teachers State-wide. It pointed out, foolishly I think, that any child who wanted sports coaching could still get it by spending their own time and money to get the benefits.

It added "The Director-General of Education deserves the support of teachers, parents and politicians, and not the almost automatic opposition which seems to greet any intelligent official attempt to mitigate the worst effects of the chronic shortage of trained teachers in this State."

The Editor got some support.

Letters, P Lambert. Heartiest congratulations on your editorial about school sport. The crocodile tears being shed about the alleged demise of high school sport make one doubt the integrity of teacher organisations. Everyone knows that school sport meant a half-day off for large numbers of teachers and children. Even when the Government offers to pay the teachers not to take the half-day off, howls of fury rend the air.

It is to be hoped that soon the Government will take a long, hard look at primary school sport, too. Work stops at lunchtime every Friday. Anyone at all interested in sport goes off in a bus to take part in inter-school sport. The remaining children waste their time in classrooms for an hour and then are driven out, reluctantly, to waste another hour in the playground.

Others saw it all differently. The writer does not seem to have much of an argument, but he adds to the fray.

Letters, E Bedford, MLA. The last two issues of the Education Gazette published by the New South Wales Department of Education have front-cover photographs showing gymnastics (May) and football (June).

Many readers of the education gazette would have taken this as a tribute to the sports programs conducted in our high schools.

We now learn that it was an obituary for school sport; or perhaps the work of a historian wanting to record the benefits of school sport for future generations who would otherwise have little idea of what they had missed because of the Government's education bungle.

Letters, Elaine Chesworth, President, Australian Council on Health, Physical Education and Recreation. Your editorial draws attention to a number of significant points concerning the teacher shortage and the emergency measures to be introduced in 1972 in an attempt to overcome the present crisis.

You express wonder at the indignation being voiced regarding the abolition of compulsory school sport which, you say, "has always been of dubious value for some students." The students to whom you refer are the less able ones in sporting activities, and it is important for the public to know that during recent years an increasing number of our schools have been rearranging their compulsory sport programs to provide equal opportunity for all students in sport time.

If sport, no matter how it is organised, becomes an optional extra, the students to whom you refer - the very ones who need physical activity and sport experience - will not be the ones to take advantage of an optional activity.

If and when the three periods of compulsory sport are discontinued in 1972, the amount of organised physical activity for high school students would be totally inadequate to develop and maintain sound general health and an acceptable level of physical fitness.

In addition, the time available would be insufficient to provide the recreational skills so necessary for people who live in present-day society.

Without compulsory sport, such a situation could only be described as a slide backwards into the "dark ages" when man understood little or nothing about the role of regular physical activity in the development of human health and welfare.

Any decision to cut three out of five, three out of four, or all three periods of organised, compulsory physical activity in school time for High School students in 1972 must be viewed as nothing short of disastrous in this day and age.

Not at all daunted, Mr Bedford has another try. Let's see if it is any better than his first,

Letters, E Bedford, MLA. Your editorial statement that compulsory sport has always been of dubious value for some students reflects a most disturbing attitude.

As a former teacher, I can assure you that **all compulsory subjects have always been of dubious value for some students**. Do you suggest that we abandon compulsory subjects altogether?

That the Director-General of Education and his staff are faced with a massive problem in the years ahead is not disputed.

Surely we are not now expected to greet as an "intelligent official attempt to mitigate the worst effects of the chronic shortage of trained teachers in this State" the Government's decision to abandon compulsory school sport.

Comment. The place of sports in school has been argued over and over since, with no definite answer. Various Governments have conducted studies and had all sorts of Committees and conferences about the matter. In fact, their reports have grown longer and longer, but to no avail.

One consideration was the growing desire to shield children from doing things that they did not want to do. Also, in contact sports, there was desire to keep the children from injury. **And** if a child wanted to do ballet and not Rugby, he could not do so. And there was the argument that if sports led to winners and losers, the loser might be damaged by recurring losses. **The arguments went on and on.**

One argument **for** compulsory sport was that it guaranteed that children would get the physical exercise from it. Also, the idea, that some held, that playing as a team prepared you for becoming a responsible citizen later in life. As I said, **the arguments went on and on.**

And that is where I leave it. I am not wise enough to offer any solution to a problem that has raged for 50 years.

SOME ANGLES ON THE SUBJECT OF ANGLING

The battle for turf in the fishing industry is as old as the hills. As soon as one problem is solved, another appears. Right here and now, swords are drawn over the supposed over-fishing of Sydney Harbour. But you will find that, if you live near an ocean or river, your own locality has its own problems.

Letters, J Taylor. There are, perhaps, 40 professional prawn-boats operating in Sydney Harbour. They fish from 6pm to about 7am, five nights a week, in an area extending from Haberfield Bay right down the Harbour as far as Clifton Gardens and beyond in the estuarine arm of Middle Harbour.

Each night, an organised boat is capable of 12 "shots," that is, immersing the heavily weighted net and dragging it about the bottom of the Harbour floor for one hour, then winching it in.

In one "shot" I counted more than 70 small bream which had perished in the net and were later cast over the side to be devoured by the gulls. These small bream are the foundation of the State Snapper Fishery and highly prized by the amateur for their sport fishing and edible qualities.

A single professional prawn-boat in one night can destroy more than 800 fish. Forty boats can destroy more than 30,000. Simple arithmetic gives us a tally of 150,000 for the week's netting activities.

The mind boggles - no fishery can support such a mortality rate, particularly when one considers that the fish which perished in the nets that night have already run the gauntlet of natural selection. They were the chosen few, and quite large enough for the vast majority to reach maturity.

As one of the 500,000 amateur anglers living on and around this potentially sterile Harbour, I exhort the State Government and the Department of Fisheries to intercede while the nucleus of a fishery still exists. Prohibit professional netting in Port Jackson proper and all its estuarine arms. Prohibit it also in the Hawkesbury River Basin, Botany Bay and Port Hacking. Then, 10 years from now, I might be fortunate enough to nail a 5lb "red" off Point Piper as my grandfather used to do.

Letters, L H Walsh. Dr Francois in his letter states that large numbers of small fish being killed by prawn trawling in Sydney Harbour has significant effect on fish population. If this is so, why is an amateur fisherman fined for catching three or four small red bream on a handline?

There do not appear to be any possible means of reconciling his statement with the law.

Letters, L Jamieson. Unfortunately, the situation is worse than described by J M Taylor. Not only do the prawners operate all night but the commercial fishermen net all day.

The scale and intensity of the netting is staggering and can only be properly appreciated by those who live on the waterfront. I have seen one small bay netted repeatedly from dawn to dusk, and the same small bay netted five times before 8.30am. Mr Willis, in attempted justification of the present policy, belittles the effect of the removal of small fish by commercial fishermen. Bearing in mind the size of the fish in question, his comments are ludicrous. But if he believes he is right, would he please answer L H Walsh, and explain why inspectors from the Fisheries Department were so busy early this year apprehending anglers with a few undersized fish? He might also tell us why we should have any minimum legal sizes for fish, why the mesh size in nets is controlled and, extrapolating, why one and all are not allowed to use nets.

A point which Mr Willis fails, or refuses, to understand is that successful angling requires a higher density of fish than intensive netting leaves. Is it too much to hope that the present administration of the State Fisheries will adopt the enlightened and progressive attitude to the sport fishery found elsewhere? Or is the lure of the levy on commercial catches (paid to the State Fisheries) too strong?

CLOTHES MAKETH THE WOMAN

Letters, A McIntyre. I was very interested in the remark of Mr Charles Lloyd Jones in his speech at the presentation of the second David Jones' Awards for Fashion Excellence: "Today's fashion inspiration more often comes from the streets."

I would go further, and say "from the gutter, or the great-grandmother's rag-bag or fancy-dress chest."

Will women come to their senses and accept only the fashions which make them look elegant and beautiful, or are they - particularly the young - going to continue to look like hideous scarecrows?

AUGUST NEWS ITEMS

Another sign that we will quit Vietnam soon. The youths who were previously drafted for National Service were required to serve 24 months. In future, this will be reduced to 18 months....

Just for interest. There are currently 45,000 men in our Army. Of these, 16,000 are doing National Service.

Eric Willis, the Chief Justice of NSW, occupies an important position. But **he is under intense fire from the Unions**. The State Industrial Commission granted **full pay to workers who were off work** through injury in the workplace....

The reason for this was that, through no fault of their own, they could not work. So, their incomes should not be reduced....

Willis opposed this saying that if the injured got full pay, there would be no incentive for them to return to work. In Parliament he critised **these workers as "genuine loafers, shirkers, and bludgers."** The Unions in reply described him as **"immoral, inhuman, dishonest, irresponsible and slanderous."** Negotiations are continuing.

There were 768 arrests in total during the tour by the South African Rugby Union Tour.

At the Australian Touring Car Championships, a 21-year-old intruder injected himself into the race. He drove onto the track from a back exit, and **did a**

full lap before stopping at the control tower, He was charged with illegally using a car.

Richard Neville **was an Australian University student who in about 1960, turned to publishing.** His main **product was** OZ magazine**, published here and in the UK. It was an irreverent funny magazine, superbly illustrated, that ruffled the feathers of all our dignitaries and authorities....**

In London, in 1971, he and two others was charged **with conspiracy and offensive literature, and found guilty, but they were released on appeal.** People who **offered him monetary aid included John Lennon, and Mick Jagger. Yoko Ono offered to "stand trial in his place."**....

The eventual suppression of the magazine left a big hole in this nation's satirical literature. **Past copies of Oz cost a fortune now in the 2020's.**

The US Government has urged 500 TV stations in America **not to show the film entitled "The Doomsday Flight."** This movie **was first shown in America** before the recent Qantas hoax, and was clearly the genesis of the model used by Brown....

In Australia, last month, a second attempt to extort money occurred here **when similar demands on an airline, Ansett, were made**. This time, no money changed hands.

MR BROWN

Mr Brown, famous for extracting $500.000 from Qantas, was really a 31-year-old labourer from Devon in England, and was here in Australia because he was on the run from British police. He devised the hoax after seeing the American movie "The Doomsday Flight" that showed almost step by step how to do it yourself. His accomplice was a marine-engineer, born in NSW.

You will remember that they had rung Qantas and said there **was a bomb on a flight that was in the air**. He gave Police enough time to locate a proto-type of the bomb in a railway locker, and said by phone that the real one would detonate at a certain height unless he electronically stopped it from doing so. Qantas and the Police decided that it was too risky to call the Brown's bluff, and quietly paid over the money in cash. The police sought Brown with fervour, and for a while seemed to be getting nowhere. It turned out that there was no bomb on the plane.

But things **were** happening. A neighbour of the accomplice noticed that this man, apparently with no prospects, suddenly had two flashy cars, and showed other signs of opulence. The neighbour told Police and they used various means to track the accomplice and Brown.

In early August, they arrested the pair, and charged them with the crime. They found a large sum, about half the missing money, in a walled-up fireplace in Brown's flat, and it was beyond doubt that the pair were guilty.

The rest of the cash has never been found. Brown was given a 15 year sentence. After seven years, he was deported back to Britain. The accomplice got seven years.

Comment. The end of this story is a bit of a disappointment. Such an audacious robbery should have a finale with car chases, shoot outs, sobbing women, and an elusive Mr Big. But there was none of this. Just a few Court hearings, and then off to gaol. **We deserve better.**

DYING IS BIG BUSINESS
The following Letter illustrates two interesting points.

Letters, L Gilbert. Someone seems determined to see Sydney well equipped with crematoriums. A few months ago Ryde Council rejected an application for the establishment of one of these enterprises in North Ryde, not far from the university. In the debate it apparently emerged that yet another was planned for the Field of Mars cemetery. The thought of three crematoriums within a radius of three miles is mind-boggling.

I have made numerous inquiries to obtain confirmation of the Field of Mars project, but beyond learning indirectly that an application was made for land (apparently another slice of the Field of Mars Reserve) I have drawn a blank.

The Field of Mars cemetery has grown steadily in recent years, gradually eroding the timber crown of the hill on which it was established. It is certainly better cared for than was the case a few years back.

It was started in the shale area, but has moved into adjoining sandstone areas. This land is rocky, uneven and sloping, in fact unsuitable for this purpose. It has been filled and terraced with imported soil, much of it lying over natural easements which drain into the adjoining reserve and creek.

Cemeteries are commercial enterprises; this one is no exception. Yet emotional and religious overtones, and a public idea of the requirements of "good taste," seem to give them an immunity from criticism that other undertakings could envy.

However, this place is steadily filling and must run out of land again. The attraction of a crematorium is obvious, if not appreciated by local residents.

We would be delighted to see a public denial that this project exists and could only interpret silence as confirmation. Our past experience has been that expansion plans have been announced with a bulldozer and falling trees.

If it is to be built, we would like to know if further encroachment on public land is contemplated. Since this area is also adjacent to a large proposed sporting complex and served by the same busy, unsuitable roads, what of the traffic?

Comment. The first point is that, again we see the growing intolerance for large projects that snaffle public lands, and pose environmental risks. As I said earlier, there were plenty of vigilantes who would resist, and a growing number of them were prepared to join resistance groups to preserve their way of life. But there was a seemingly endless number of projects that were being initiated by inventive and money-driven entrepreneurs who kept popping up with their version of what's good for the community.

The second point is that the number of cremations in Australia started to increase about the early seventies. Before that, death meant that most people were **buried**. After that, the percentage of cremations increased by about one percent a year, so that by the year 2,000, half of the deaths were serviced by crematoria.

By 2014, the were 850 cemetries in NSW, and 50 crematoria. But many of the cemetries were in virtual paddocks, often with cattle grazing, that accounted for small numbers. The crematoria were much larger and were concentrated on the edges of cities, and often adorned with large lawns and elaborate chapels.

The above Letter gives notice that the search for large, professional, profitable tracts of land was suddenly accelerating in Sydney, and elsewhere.

Comment. The falling percentage of burials fits in with the fall in religious observance. Simply put, was the practice of burning the body consistent with resurrection after death? There is little logic in this question, but it was one that often preyed on the minds of grieving relatives.

WAYS TO BE A GOOD SCOUT
Surely, everyone agrees that our boy scouts and girl guides are being trained in all the good virtues. Surely, everyone thinks that all the motives of those who train them are beyond reproach.

Apparently this is not the case. The person below has found something sinister in the Bob-a-Job campaign. It is not just that children expect adults to reward them for doing next to nothing. That would not be consistent with the ethos of the Movement. It is more sinister than that.

August 7, W Ords. As parents of a 12-year-old Sea Scout, we were last week presented with a circular letter relating to Scout Job Week, previously known as "Bob a Job" week.

One does not wish to attack the aims and plans of the Scouting movement to provide alpine adventure centres, rock-climbing centres and water training centres. In fact they are aims worthy of community and parental support.

However, it is wrong in principle that provision of these amenities should result from an induced competitive effort from each Scout, whereby he is presented with either a purple, silver or gold award relative to the amount earned.

It is disturbing to note that Scout Job Week has been degraded by becoming subject to a three-tier award system for effort. This is entirely wrong in concept because all Scouts, no matter how willing, would not have equal opportunity to earn the high amounts NSW Chief Commissioner Pilz wishes them to achieve.

May we ask the Chief Commissioner to re-think next year, when the time comes for Scout Job Week. These boys should not be encouraged in "one-upmanship" which the present award system generates. Development of boys' natural enthusiasm towards working for the group is all that is needed - young people are willing workers when given the right kind of inspiration.

But not everyone agrees. In fact, quite a few. I enclose a typical response.

Letters, Alan Black. The boys in the scout movement are not pampered little violets who shrink away from the world. They can stand quite a lot of pressure. They can compete, or not compete, as they choose.

The Ords think their delicate little psychies will be permanently damaged by an optional competition. Instead, they will get outside their protected communities that most of them live in, and get some experience in the real world that will improve their ability to mix in society.

The Ords obviously think that the Movement is worthwhile. So I ask them to also think about the money that is needed to send the boys to the mountains and so on. If there was no effective Bob-a-Job programme, where would this money come from?

Letters, R Thompson, Area Commissioner, Australian Boy Scouts Association. To your correspondents W Ord, who commented on the endeavour awards introduced with this year's Scout Job Week, I would like to point out that all we expect of the individual Scout and Cub is that he does his best in carrying out as many jobs as he is able, in relation to his family and school commitments.

Because many Scouts are exceeding what they earned only two years ago, these awards have been introduced to recognise those boys who make the extra effort, in the same way that they can earn achievement and proficiency badges through additional work in passing tests and completing projects.

Let me hasten to assure your correspondents that this year, as in past job weeks, all we ask is that the boy does his best and that there is absolutely no restriction of scouting facilities and fellowship for those boys who for good reasons are not able to complete as many jobs as their fellow Scouts.

SAVE THE ROO

World-wide sales of kangaroo meat were booming in restaurants. Sales in London were particularly strong where the condescending Poms made many references to Australians eating their national symbol. Pressure had been building up to stop the trade in roo meat and furs, and in December last year some States brought down regulations to do this, with a few other Aussie native products thrown in as well.

One retailer of skin products in Sydney complained that his sales of ladies handbags made from the leather of cane toad hides had dried up. He described then as having "croaked."

ON THE NOSE

Letters, G Birdsall. In reference to your recent editorial, entitled "Sweet smell of success":

We are rather surprised that you have once again inferred that tanneries contribute to offensive smells. We believe that you are confusing tanneries with other industries due to lack of up-to-date knowledge of the industry.

There are no tanneries situated on O'Riordan Street or Old Botany Road. Are you aware of this?

Our tannery, which is situated on Wentworth Avenue and Beresford Street, Mascot, is one of the two tanneries in Mascot. The majority are situated in Botany.

We welcome you to visit our tannery, smell it at first hand and then give due recognition to this much maligned industry.

Comment. The smell of the tannery from the road to the airport was legendary. It filled the area around it, and filled all cars for a distance of a mile on either side of it.

Despite the protests of Mr Birdsall, I am firmly convinced that the smell **did** come from the tannery there.

LONG-AWAITED NEWS FROM THE CATTERY

Letters, John Henney. Mr Gunston's piece, "Can animals see colour?", seems to me to contain a trifle too much dogmatism.

"We know that almost all the mammals, with the notable exceptions of the apes and monkeys, do not see colours at all." What is the evidence for this amazing statement, and who is "we"?

The mammals - dogs, cats, buffaloes, rhinoceroses, elephants and horses - have eyes structured the same way as man's. These animals possess the same rods and cones in the eyes, the same optic nerve, the same efferent and afferent nerves, and it is in the same part of the brain where the sensation of perception is somehow changed into the picture of what we imagine we are seeing out there.

There is no evidence to lead us to believe that what another mammal sees is different in colour from what a man sees. It might well be that what Mr Gaston sees as blue his cat might see as red, but to claim that the cat cannot sense colour is taking too great a liberty with probability.

We see what we see because our eyes are what they are, and man's eyes closely resemble the eyes of the other mammals.

DON'T CALL IT PING PONG

A controversy erupted over the place of table tennis in the world, and whether it deserved a place in the Olympics. Various authorities were saying that the game was nothing more than ping-pong. Why should such an unchallenging sport be afforded Olympic statues when much more vigorous sports were not?

Then came the hub of the issue. The Chinese would win all the medals awarded for table tennis. That helped their medal count, which at this stage was on the verge of becoming more important than the events themselves.

So, the game was developing strong political overtones. Each of the major nations in the world were doing all they could to establish themselves as superior to all others.

How could a country prove this if its medal count at the Olympics was too low?

The reply below captures a little of the argument that was raging. He says that table tennis is a proper sport. And flirts with the notion of the game becoming an international political pawn.

Letters, L Bennett, English Table Tennis Association. During a news session from a Sydney television station providing political commentary on the significance of the invitation of national table tennis teams, including that of USA, to Communist China, I had to suffer scornful references to table tennis as ping-pong.

The connotation of the modern sport of table tennis as pat-ball parlour ping-pong is as ill-conceived as it is slighting. For the past 40 years, international table tennis has attracted spectators in thousands through the world, requiring athletic physical agility and immense proficiency from its exponents. Anyone privileged to watch the great Victor Baran at his best before WWII would retain an indelible memory of skill and grace.

Since these days sport has become virtually a component of politics, it is timely to recall that many years ago the International Table Tennis Federation abolished distinction between professional and amateur players and refused South Africa full membership because of its discrimination against non-white players.

Now the liberal policy of the Federation of encouraging all peoples to compete in friendship together has led to a signal and important recognition by Communist China which could lead to an improvement in international understanding.

It is certainly not the moment to belittle table tennis by the derisive equation with ping-pong.

CRITICISM OF NURSING STAFF

The Letters column in the newspapers often carried comments on the dictatorial performances of hospital matrons. They were often referred to standing aloof from patients and family, of bullying nurses, and of being out of touch with what the community wanted.

Some of this criticism has rubbed of onto the ordinary nurse in the ward. Their performance on the job is not criticised, but rather their aloofness and an apparent lack of sympathy for patients.

The Letter below offers a response.

Letters, S Orr. As a trained nursing sister I would like to add some comments to the unending stream about the behaviour of nurses.

These girls do not seek glory for having chosen their profession - all they ask is consideration and average courtesy from their patients. Student nurses are too often considered by those in their care as capable of only the most menial tasks, and patients who are the most unpleasant are frequently the ones who complain at great length about the way these girls treat them.

All young nurses set out initially to help, please and comfort their patients, but often this becomes virtually impossible when they are faced with people who have been hospitalised many times, have chronic illnesses and choose to be rude, demanding and usually self-appointed experts on their own treatment. These patients, in my experience, are invariably female, often middle-aged and always difficult for an 18-year-old student to handle.

I believe that a pleasant, co-operative patient rarely receives anything but perfectly reasonable treatment from the nursing staff. There can be clashes of personality, because we cannot all like all the people with whom we come into contact.

Comment. Patients and families were quick to support the nurses. They generally took the line that the complaints against them were unjustified, but given the certainty that they would still happen, the nurses should ignore them and continue to stay, to quote one Letter, "as sweet as you are".

SEPTEMBER NEWS ITEMS

A large medical conference in Washington was told, by reputable **doctors from Israel**, that **the common cold could be cured by the chilling of big toes.** There is apparently a nervous system connection between the big toes and the nose, so that cooling dries up the nostrils and kills the cold....

Doctors were sceptical, but did not reject the report out of hand. One Australian doctor said that maybe it would indeed give temporary relief to the symptoms, but doubted that it would kill the virus.....

The Israelis have applied for a patent for their toe chiller.

Some comforting news from Washington. The Chinese have developed missiles that can **carry nuclear bombs 1,000 miles.** Previously it was a long way behind the US and Russia, but now it is **closing the gap quickly in the arms race.**...

Comment. Healthy competition is good for the world.

As a feature to please the crowd of 10,000 after the big annual City-to-Surf Fun Run, ten **parachutists were to free-fall from the sky onto Bondi Beach**....

Sudden changes in the wind caused **one woman to miss the beach and land into the raging sea.** She got progressively more tangled in her chute, and sank. Several men attempted to save her, as the crowd watched, but it took 20 minutes to drag her out. **She died later in hospital.**

Fireworks will be banned in Queensland from now. Only big fireworks displays will be allowed. **Comment. Other States followed. Pity. The lunatic tail is wagging the dog again.**

Two sisters, and their eight children, were shot and killed in a cottage in the Adelaide Hills. The victims were asleep when a man, the husband of one of the sisters, **clubbed them with a large rubber mallet. He then shot them** with a single-shot .22 rifle. He was charged with murder.

The planned cricket tour of Australia by the South African side has been called off. Sir Donald Bradman commented that "we did not want to drag politics into cricket, but South Africa clearly does."

Nikita Khrushchev, former leader of the Communist Party in the USSR, **has died.** He was ousted in 1964, and has lived in some isolation ever since. **He will not be given a State Funeral** which indicates that all is not forgiven by the **current leadership.**

Ten people were killed and 60 were injured **in a pile-up on England's M6 Motorway** near London. Fog and slippery conditions were the cause. Such crashes have occurred in the past, but this was a record.

Harry Miller, a well-known musical identity is Sydney is trying, in the Equity Court, to stop Sydney's Loreto Convent and St Aloyisius College from performing extracts from *Jesus Christ Superstar* at **their Annual School Concert.**

CRICKET TOUR IS OFF

The Board of Control of Cricket Australia announced that the tour of South Africa has been cancelled. A Press release from Sir Donald Bradman said:

"The board faced the unenviable situation that whatever decision it made would meet with the displeasure of a large percentage of the people, but it could not let that factor influence it in coming to a decision.

"It weighed carefully the views expressed by responsible Australian authorities, including political leaders, union officials, church dignitaries, police commissioners, ground authorities, administrative officials and others.

"There could be no doubt the tour would set up internal bitterness between rival groups and demonstrations on a large scale would be inevitable.

"The police would be called upon to provide massive and prolonged protection at matches and elsewhere.

"The board has complete confidence in the ability and willingness of the police forces to maintain law and order, but had to question whether it was reasonable in the circumstances to ask these men to undergo the severe ordeal which would be demanded of them to enable cricket to be played in peace, and at the same time other members of the public being deprived of their services.

"Also, was it reasonable to expect international cricketers to perform under the trying circumstances which would prevail?

"Having deeply considered all these matters, the Board felt it was in the best interests of Australia, of the game of cricket and all those associated with it, that the tour should not take place."

Comment. The decision means that New Zealand is the only remaining nation that will play cricket with South Africa.

One of the consequences of this will be that South African cricketers will certainly go to other nations to earn a living, and make their names. Australia and England will get the benefits of this, but it means that South Africa will lose its best players for years to come.

Almost all other countries **in all other sports** have decided to black-list the South African sports teams . **It is hard to know what good this did. I don't think any one will ever really know.**

But there was another side to the matter. The Editor of the *SMH* saw it as a question of law and order. He said that people had the right to demonstrate, but they must do it within the law. He believed that the Board should not back down in the face of violence, and he believed that the majority of Australians would agree on that.

Even those who disapproved of this tour, certainly a substantial section of the community, must feel perturbed at this triumph of force and authoritarianism. The authoritarian minority naturally will be elated. They will see the Board's decision as a vindication of their ugly tactics against the South African footballers.

They may see it as encouragement to seek out other areas where they can impose their wishes and, under a smokescreen of self-righteousness, savour a vicious sense of power. If so, they will misread the temper of the Australian people, who are heartily sick of the coercive tactics of minorities, regardless of the merits - if they exist - of their pretended causes. From now on we can expect far less tolerance of the demonstrator who sets his ideas and actions above the law.

There was a lot of support for the Editor.

Letters, W Herniman. Even to me - I hold no brief for apartheid - the decision to cancel the South African tour is disappointing.

It is an old-established principle of our law that if one person has rights (eg. to protest) he must use them in such a manner as not to infringe the rights of his neighbour (eg. to watch a cricket match on private property in peace).

To me, the decision of the board of control does not represent a statesmanlike cancellation, but is rather a surrender to the lawlessness of a very small minority.

This breakdown in the rule of law represents a triumph for expediency over principle, and cannot be otherwise than disturbing; where will it lead?

There was another argument that **said that if we lay** the boot into South Africa for racial discrimination, then it could be that **other nations will lay the boot into us for the same reason**.

Letters, Eric Small. Australia's performance on its treatment of blacks is little different from that of South Africa. Look at housing, at education, at financial assistance, at position before the law, at the numbers in prison, at the bans on grog, and so many other areas. In all cases, our blacks are treated abominably.

Anyone from abroad looking at Australia can see that there is one rule, and one system of care, for the whites, and another for the blacks.

Before we punish South Africa for being racist, we should fix our own situation, because if we don't we might find that it is us who are being black-listed along with South Africa.

Letters, Fair go mate. The difference here is that in Australia we have been bending over backwards for 10 years to do something for our blacks. Our Governments are trying everything, with the support of the populace, to improve things in all areas.

Our problem is that our blacks come from a different world, with a long culture very different from ours. To ask them to change their ways is for them, and for us white people, a most difficult problem.

But here in Australia we are trying to do this. And we are slowly succeeding. **In South Africa, it seems that they are instead turning the clock back and consolidating a system of repression and disadvantage.**

Given our progress, however slow, the overseas judge **should praise, and not condemn, us.**

Comment. This ban on South African sport, and also the wider system of Apartheid, went on for another decade and even longer in some matters.

STRIKES GALORE

I have mentioned in a few places that strikes were the bane of every housewife and family in the nation. There were strikes everywhere, all the time. Big ones, small ones, some were just a walk off the job for half a day, some were for a few weeks and stopped the nation. All Governments, State and Federal, Liberal and Labor, **were frightened to seriously tackle the Union movement,**and indeed stayed out of the fray until Bob Hawke and Paul Keating brought in their Accord in 1983.

I will not go into detail of the annoyance and frustration that strikes brought to the nation. What I will do is give you a *SMH* editorial that illustrates some of ways that strikes started and proceeded.

SMH Editorial. It is no more than a domestic, kitchen-sink squabble between a construction gang foreman and two workmen in his gang. The foreman did not like the attitude of the two employees and the men reciprocated. As a result the foreman sacked the two men and the union objected. Because of this monumental clash of personalities on one small construction gang at Narrabeen, 11,500 Water Board employees have been on strike, many for more than a week, 150 million gallons of raw sewage has been pouring into the sea from Sydney's ocean outfalls each day polluting the beaches, and 250 householders cut off from water by broken mains have been reduced to carting supplies in buckets and saucepans.

If the implications were not so serious we might all be having a big laugh over this comic Water Board opera. The whole sorry episode says little for the staff relations of the Board and less for the responsibility of the Water Board Employees' Union. The industrial relations expertise of both are revealed as lamentable. The dispute could and should have been settled internally before it got out of hand. The strike having reached the State conciliation courts, this machinery proved almost equally ineffective. It has taken a week for the Conciliation Commissioner to make an order which provides for the temporary reinstatement of the dismissed men while the issue goes before a higher court.

COMPULSORY VOTING IN LOCAL ELECTIONS

Voting in Federal and State elections has been compulsory for a long time. We all accept it as normal. But in most States, when it comes to local elections, voters in 1971 were free to vote or not free, as they choose.

Lately though there has bee a lot of talk about making voting mandatory at the local level.

Letters, A Mander. Since last Saturday's local elections some of the candidates - defeated candidates, of course

- have been urging that compulsory voting should be restored.

Whenever voting is compulsory in any election, a considerable proportion of all votes counted are "don't care" votes. In other words, they are the votes cast by persons who take so little interest in the matter that they would not vote, unless legally obliged to do so.

From the standpoint of political democracy, what can such votes be worth? It is true that everyone may be entitled to participate in a democratic election. But being entitled to do something has a different meaning from being compelled to do it.

And in any case, surely "participation in a democratic election" does not consist merely in the physical act of making marks on a ballot paper. Essentially, it lies in an individual taking enough interest in the matter to lead to his making a deliberate choice or decision - which he expresses through his vote.

Therefore, such persons as either know nothing or care nothing about the issues at stake, who are indeed so uninterested that they would not, without compulsion, even put themselves to the small trouble of going to the polling booth - surely they cannot be described, in any meaningful sense, as "participating" in a democratic election.

Nor can their votes be described as democratic votes. For how could they be regarded as expressing the "will" of the voters? They have no will to express on the subject; they are completely uninterested, as shown by the fact that they don't even want to vote. What a confession of weakness for any candidate to make: that he needs those votes to put him in.

Comment. The question of compulsory voting in Federal and State elections has largely gone off the agenda in Australia. Around the time of Federation in 1901, it was of great concern, but interest fell away, and now it is generally taken as a given.

But there are still some dissidents.

Letters, Alfread Deaken. In America, about 30 per cent of the people vote in Presidential elections, and about 80 per cent of them always vote for the same party each time. It can hardly be said that their votes represent the will of the entire nation. They might crow that democracy is grand, but no one can claim that all the people are represented.

Turning to Australia , the whole idea of democracy is crazy. Half the population has an IQ less than 100. Do we want the lower half to choose our leaders? Do we want them to set national policy? Most people vote for what their Dad did, and their interest in policy issues is negligible. They vote out of envy and spite, with imperfect or no knowledge. Or they turn the whole process into a gender issue.

What a way to run a country. The only way to get responsibility is to give the vote to property owners, broadly defined, and to people with educational qualifications, or status, again suitably defined. For those too young to have the above, let them wait until they are old enough to do some balanced thinking.

THE 51st STATE OF THE USA

A citizen of the Armidale University had an interesting suggestion.

Letters, J Pigram, University of New England. The recent comments of Mr Heath portraying Britain's entry into Europe as a response to the withdrawal of protective US influence suggest that a somewhat similar pragmatic philosophy might be in Australia's interests. The suggestion is that "If you can't beat 'em, join 'em"; that Australia and New Zealand should seek full Statehood with the USA as the 52nd and 53rd States.

Many people probably believe that this is already a fact, but before patriotically minded readers have apoplexy, it might be as well to consider some advantages which come readily to mind from political union with our "great and powerful friends."

From the defence point of view, ANZUS would immediately become redundant, our forward payments for the F111 would be credited to our State account and R and R leave would continue to swell the takings of the fleshpots of Kings Cross.

Economically, we should gain from parity with the US dollar and from an absence of embargoes, quotas and surcharges on our trade. The Qantas problem would immediately be solved by absorption into Pan-Am or American Airlines.

In the political arena, our leaders would be cut down to a size more appropriate to their ability and international standing, and as congressmen could freely visit the now-secret US bases.

Side benefits would include the ending of the search for a new anthem and flag and the extension of Ralph Nader's activities to the "South Pacific States." The liberated could smoke pot and view "Oh! Calcutta!" at their leisure and even the apartheid "do-gooders" could have their sincerity tested with the arrival of the first boatload of Negro immigrants for the "New California."

Already a good deal of this country's land and resources has been sold to American interests, while, culturally, the younger generation, at least, has long since lost its Australian identity. Given another few years of "Sesame Street," "Mod Squad," etc, the process of Americanisation should be complete. On balance, complete political union would seem a logical extension of this trend and a worthwhile issue for Mr McMahon (Governor-elect?) to raise with President Nixon on his forthcoming pilgrimage.

OCTOBER NEWS ITEMS

In the Northern Territory, police are searching for an unknown **crocodile bomber**. At Timber Creek, 300 miles south of Darwin, some person each night detonates a bomb in the many local rivers, and thereby kills crocodiles. He takes their skins, and apparently sells them. **They bring $3 an inch from dealers.**

Filipino boxer Alberto Jangalay **died last night** after being knocked out in the eighth round of a scheduled 10-round **fight at Brisbane's Festival Hall**.

In NSW, 25 persons were killed on the road over the **long week-end period**. This was the first time that the wearing of **seat belts was mandatory**. Police emphasise that most of those killed were **not** wearing belts.

Not to be denied. Cricket lovers in Australia will not be denied their summer cricket. Instead of a South African tour, **a Rest-of-the-World team,** from the major cricketing nations, will tour. It will have 17 players from South Africa, England, India, Pakistan, West Indies, and New Zealand. **The Captain will be Gary Sobers, a very black man.**

Times are changing. Emperor Hirohito of Japan will fly to England for a State visit. It is designed to settle animosities that remain after the war. British Veteran's Associations object to the visit, but will not publicly protest. They will instead turn off their television sets whenever the Emperor comes on....

Another change imminent is the proposed visit of US President Richard Nixon to Communist China. This is proposed now by Henry Kissinger, Nixon's adviser....

What a turn-round from the hatred and contempt of a year ago.

The Victorian Minister for Labour and Industry has warned investors that **pyramid schemes present quite a sizeable risk**. This way to sell cosmetics and detergents has proved to be "a practice that **could not be allowed to continue unabated.**" He promised to **introduce restraining legislation** unless the schemes cleaned up their acts. His was **the first State** to speak up on this matter. The others acted very soon after.

A concert at the **NSW Conservatorium of Music** was stopped by a Director when two young pianists were playing. The Director walked onto the stage during a performance, **closed the lid, and turned the key in the lock**. He said that they were putting music-stands and kitchen utensils into the piano, and at one stage dived full length onto the keyboard. **He intervened to protect the valuable Steinway grand piano.**

Six girl trapeze artists were badly injured when a platform of which they were performing crashed to the earth. They fell with it, and **three ended with broken spines**, and the others had spinal and pelvic injuries.

They were performing in the **"Disney on Parade" Show** in front of 500 people. Several women in the audience collapsed.

CHINA INTO UN, AT LAST?

China and the US have been at logger-heads since the new government of Red China was established in 1949. Apart from the many disputes over policy matters, the reason behind the disagreements is that the US is Capitalist, and China is Communist. Say no more.

Taiwan is an island off the coast of China, and it is a member of the coveted United Nations. China and Taiwan have played no-speaks for 23 years. China wants to join the UN, but is always blocked by the US. It seems that it might squeak in, by a change in the voting procedure.

The prospect of this brought forward these Letters

Letters, C Mackerras, Dept of Far Eastern History, ANU, and 104 Others. In November, 1970, the United Nations voted by a simple majority to admit the People's Republic of China. This vote was nullified by a resolution, supported by countries like Australia, demanding a two-thirds majority for China's admission.

Since last year, the movement towards diplomatic recognition of Peking has gathered momentum. Many countries, such as Chile, Austria, and Turkey, have established Embassies in Peking or announced their intention of doing so. Even the United States is moving in this direction, and the explicit aim of Nixon's forthcoming trip to China is the normalisation of relations between the two countries.

We call on the Australian Government this year to vote unequivocally for the seating of China in both the General Assembly and the Security Council of the UN, so that the Chinese people can take their rightful place, which has been denied them for over 20 years.

We deplore what amounts to a decision to try to delay the seating of China by making the expulsion of Taiwan "an important question" requiring a two-thirds majority.

We call on our Government immediately to establish diplomatic relations with the People's Republic of China following the Canadian formula. This would be in the interests of the people of Australia, the people of China and the peace and security of the world.

Letters, D Darby, MLA. How vociferously Colin Mackerras and 104 others demand, in the interests of the peace and security of the world, that Australia should give absolute recognition to the regime which calls itself the People's Republic of China.

If I were to assert that the Peiping Government seized and maintains its power unconstitutionally, undemocratically and so forth, Mr Mackerras would probably not agree.

If I were to say that, if Red China was able to invade Taiwan, millions of people would be slaughtered and a vital bastion protecting Australia from Communist aggression destroyed, Mr Mackerras might well assert that Peiping has no vicious overseas ambitions at all. He might be able to find a quotation from Mao's thoughts to counter the hundreds that I could cite.

I wonder if it is possible for Mr Mackerras and I to agree on one simple and easily determined formula: We could jointly declare that Australia must refuse to recognise as a member of the United Nations any Government which prevents its nationals from leaving their homelands as free peoples.

BRITS JOIN THE COMMON MARKET

The British Government voted to join the European Common Market. This of course means hard times for Australian sellers who, up to now, have had something of a captive audience for their products, especially in agriculture.

But the result was expected, and many Australian producers have already established markets for their products in Asia and elsewhere.

Comment. Almost 50 years later, in 2020, after a few years of near chaos in Britain, the Brits seem to be about to withdraw from the Common Market. And ironically, they are in serious talks with our own fair nation to revive some form of Empire Preferences.

Maybe we will revive the Bundles for Britain scheme that was such a success in the War.

STOP THE STRIKES

One Letter has a simple solution to the problem of strikes.

Letters, W Chando. The Labor member for Wentworthville, Mr Quinn, says that it could take three weeks to arrange a secret ballot.

Evidently Mr Quinn assumes that the vote could not be taken without elaborate printing and other arrangements. Of course, this is not so. Workers could use their pay envelopes to record yes or no to a strike proposal. Before placing their vote in the ballot box they would tear off portion of the envelope bearing their names and thus preserve secrecy. The pay envelopes would bear a stamp and date to ensure that there would be no duplication of votes.

Booths at the exits would be provided to enable workers to record their votes, or ballot boxes policed by a member of the management and union handily placed.

The whole procedure would take but a few minutes.

Comment. Indeed it does seem simple.

Letters, M Zabriesky. The program of the so-called militant trade-unions can be summed up in one simple sentence: "Less and less work for more and more money and to hell with the country!"

Should what they regard (and work for) as their "ultimate goal" come true, they will discover to their shocked surprise that they will have to do more and more work for less and less money. Protests are out! Strikes are out! Opinions are out! And if you don't like it, off with you to one of the hundreds of labour camps.

I know it. I saw it. I come from Poland.

NURSING HOMES

Obviously, the bulk of older people were not able to pay for the care they needed when they reached the stage where they could not care for themselves. Our governments, Federal and State, helped out by providing pensions of various kinds, and they provided hospital beds and care for some. And they subsidised the fees charged if the patient went to a private nursing home.

There was endless demand for the free hospital beds, but they could not cope with the demand. This is where the private nursing home came in. They took in this overflow, they provided a small number of free beds, and charged fees for the remainder .

These were not charitable organisations. They were putting in their money, and they wanted a return. Governments helped out a lot here by subsidising the patients. In the first week of October, the Federal Government announced a big increase in this subsidy.

But far from being satisfied, hundreds of Letters flooded into the *SMH* complaining about the faults in the system, and some of them proposed solutions. The correspondence on the matter went on for the entire month, so in the report below, I can only refer to some of the most-repeated themes from the sanest of Letters and opinions.

THE LEAD FROM WHITLAM

Gough Whitlam, Labor Leader, was the first cab off the rank. He said that:

"Incontinent patients are left lying in wet beds or in beds stuffed with newspapers.

"Potentially alert patients sit by their bedsides day after day without occupation or entertainment and are served meals on their knees or their beds.

"Profitable patients are trafficked between unscrupulous proprietors with total disregard for human dignity.

"Unprofitable ones are kept bedridden by over-sedation to qualify them for Commonwealth benefits at the intensive care rate."

Private nursing homes providing an acceptable standard of care were being forced to either lower these standards or charge fees their patients could not afford.

This week's impetuous announcement of higher benefits had been concerned with the welfare not of patients but of proprietors.

Letters, Bridget Gilling, Administrator, North Sydney Community Service. Some private convalescent homes are good but most patients on low incomes receive poor to diabolically bad care in the rest homes (a cruel joke, this) which take them on sufferance. In return, pensioners have to pay their entire pension, leaving them absolute paupers, unable to buy anything for themselves except by someone else's charity.

Letters, (Miss) E Armstrong, President, Australian association for Geriatric Nursing Care. Quoting a prominent geriatrician from 1967: "I believe there is no justification for regarding private proprietary institutions as lacking in nobility of purpose and therefore somehow inferior. Many are housed in modern, clean premises, staffed by competent, dedicated people and provide acceptable basic care. 'Proprietary' is not synonymous with 'sub-standard' any more than 'non-profit' is a synonym for 'quality'."

Letters, (Miss) Joan Short, Senior Social Worker, Sydney Hospital. In accepting admission on a permanent basis to an institution of any kind, a patient relinquishes much of that personal independence so important to any citizen. When, in addition, he must pay the whole of his pension to a private nursing home and depend on the generosity of the matron for the purchase of even the smallest item for personal use, he is robbed of the last shreds of human dignity.

Letters, (Miss) D Frazer, Social Worker in Charge, St Vincent's Hospital. With other correspondents, I deplore the existing situation where people of limited means, usually only the Commonwealth pension, are forced to accept what is virtually the only recourse available to them - nursing care in institutions run for profit.

Many such people have no option but to pay the whole of their pension for the right to remain in these homes. If the subsidy or the pension is increased, the patient rarely benefits as the increments are swallowed up in increased fees.

To be in an institution, no matter how attractive or competently run, without one cent to oneself, to be unable to buy a postage stamp or to choose one's newspaper, reduces the worth and dignity of the individual to a degree which should be intolerable in any civilised society, and particularly in a country which has taken pride in its social welfare programs.

Social workers throughout Australia, particularly those in public hospitals, have been aware of this intolerable situation for some time. Since the introduction of the Intensive Care Subsidy (1969) a committee has prepared material for presentation to the Commonwealth Government through the Australian Council of Social Service. The recent legislation providing increased subsidies seems to indicate the report has made little or no impact.

The time is long overdue for social workers to be represented at the policy-making level when social welfare legislation is proposed.

These charges were rebutted by the Director of the Private Nursing Homes of Australia.

Letters, L Farrar, Director, Private Hospitals and Nursing Homes' Association of Australia. The extreme nature of his statements entirely ignores the factual situation that the standards of these institutions have greatly improved over past years. The majority provide standards and service equal to those of any country in the world. They are subjected to regular inspections by competent officers of both Commonwealth and State departments of health to ensure that patients are at all times accorded the best possible attention in a congenial environment and are subject to competent medical and nursing care.

If Mr Whitlam has personal proof of "unscrupulous proprietors trafficking in patients," or "over-sedation" and other complaints which his statement credits to his unnamed informers, he has a public duty to report those facts to the appropriate authorities for their immediate investigation and correction.

OTHER CRITICISM OF OLDER CARE

One Reader was appalled by the proposal to erect two 30-story towers at a Sydney Suburb to house the elderly.

Letters, T Balfour. While the rest of the world is striving to reduce social alienation and institutionalisation of any segment of the community, the commission, blissfully ignoring all experience, plan to house a mass of society's least mobile members within the confines of a "grand scheme," inviting personal withdrawal and despair.

People who have lived in inner suburbs have grown attached to the variety of life they contain and to the housing forms represented there. Intense social interchange from street level front verandas may be one of the bases of the community experience.

What, then, is the point of providing high-rise units to replace that housing, if the whole exercise is supposed to be based on sociological considerations? It is irrelevant that the flats are within three miles of the GPO: they might as well be at Green Valley.

Several readers proposed half-way houses that would offer services for those who need care, but were capable of some tasks.

There were suggestions that subsidies could be given to families for the building of effectively granny flats that would allow persons to stay longer in the home environment. There was a call from the Editor of the *SMH* to improve the scrutiny of the Homes, and to guarantee the moneys they were receiving in grants and subsidies were properly spent.

This lady below would certainly agree with this.

Letters, (Mrs) C Butler. It is not always possible for an inspector of nursing homes to discover the real situation. A visit at night might uncover startling facts.

I have been a patient in two convalescent hospitals. A charming matron owned an attractive one, which provided excellent meals and was very clean. However, there was no supervision at night. The sister-in-charge became drunk and fell on the floor.

In another convalescent hospital, the night sister went the rounds asking the patients what pills they would like. Bed pans were not given when requested and if an accident occurred the patient was admonished.

Walking exercise to strengthen muscles was rarely given and there was no mental (except for TV) or physical occupation provided or encouraged.

Not all nursing homes are the same but these I experienced myself.

WERE FEES EXCESSIVE?

There were claims that the owners were profiteering, were making heaps by poor service levels, and skimping on everything. There were a few voices who pointed out that, though a few homes were like this, the majority were not.

Others rebutted the charges by saying that the Homes had every right to make a profit. **Others said no one should be allowed to make money out of caring for the aged.** Would you offer up your money without some reward?

A few fees and charges were in fact regulated by Governments that delighted in cancelling licences if there were irregularities. Therefore, they went on, there could be no chance of overcharging. (**Comment.** Really?)

The more serious complaint was that the Governments had increased subsidies, but **the Homes had just raised their charges** to recoup the same amount. One lone writer agreed with this, but added that many of the Homes needed fee increases to stay in business.

WHO WAS RAISING CAIN?

The most vocal group were Social Workers from large Sydney Hospitals. They agreed that there were some rogue Homes, but they were few in number. They were unanimous that most of the charges laid against the Homes were exaggerated and that the press had presented a picture that was far from balance.

Several expressed the view that Social Workers and doctors and nurses all had consciences, and genuinely felt for the inmates. That meant that if they started our working in a sub-standard home, they would quickly walk out when they realised this. Staff turnover, they said, was a measure of the standard of care.

Comment. We all know that there is a limit to the sum of money that can be spent on any one thing. Over the many years of writing these books, it seems that the spending on the aged always falls below a fair share.

Someone else can always argue that the total sum has risen all the time, and that so too has the sum paid to the elderly. On balance I can see that the lot of the elderly has improved over the years. That is a good thing. I just wish that more money could be found to make even greater improvements.

Curiously, though, the two countries may have come closer together **in 1971, and might even start to talk to each other**. Despite their disagreement over Taiwan.

NOVEMBER NEWS ITEMS

Rainfall in Sydney for the month of October was **the lowest on records that go back 112 years. But Melbourne had its wettest month since 1963.**

A party of 13 persons arrived at Sydney airport. There was nothing unusual about that, Some of them were jugglers. Again, nothing special about that. But one of the party was Naheb Savri. And she was described to officials as the **world's best belly dancer.** That was unusual. So the officials asked her to prove that she was good. **She did.** The officials could not say she was the world's best, but **they thought she was "pretty good".**

Golfer Jack Nicklaus won the Australia Open by a margin of eight strokes. His score for the four rounds was 19 under par. It was Nicklaus' third win in the Open.

The Melbourne Cup will close down the nation for a few hours on Tuesday. My tip is for *Tails*...

The new Sydney TAB system will have its first test when it takes its first bets on the race....

New York's new TAB will be operating on the Cup for the first time. *Ken Howard*, Australia's most famous caller, **will broadcast to an audience of 100 million** around the world.

A Melbourne mother of two died yesterday in a Melbourne hospital. She had been walking along a suburban road and was **bitten by a tiger snake**.

NSW will probably introduce a new measure that will **require the licensing of either guns or gun-owners**. In either case, it will try to move in step with Victoria. That would be the first attempt in getting **uniform gun-ownership laws across the nation**.

The number of US troops in Vietnam has dropped below **200,000. Three years ago the number was 540,000.**

Silver Knight **won the Cup.**

Reports from the US said that American interests were hopeful of **buying Australia's Simpson Desert** at 20 cents an acre. Our own Department of the Interior was **flooded with 813 applications by people from Oz** who wanted to get in on the action. **The Desert, as it turned out, was not for sale.**

The NSW Minister for Transport reminded the public that the new seat belt laws required that they be properly adjusted and securely fastened. **This means that they may not be worn loosely.** To do so is an offence, and will result in fines.

Assembled Bishops of the Roman Catholic Church have voted to **retain celibacy for themselves and their priests**. The voting was 168 for, and 34 against. **The mainly younger priests did not get a vote.**

Tasmanian Parliament has enacted laws that provide for *expenses* to be reclaimed in some cases for rescues carried out at sea. It also provided for fines of $1,000 for a person with a boat **who refuses to go to the rescue of persons in distress**.

NEWS FROM THE BALLET

I enclose this snippet to ward off any suggestions that I am a complete barbarian. Really, I suppose, you might get this impression because I have almost finished this book, and have not mentioned the arts, ballet, music, and other arty-crafty matters.

So now I will rectify that. The famous Russian dancer, Rodolf Nureyev, is in Sydney for a brief season and then off to Melbourne for the filming of his own version of *Don Quixote*. His biggest complaint about life is that he flies into an interesting city, then performs, and leaves without seeing anything.

So, there, my friends. I am not a philistine.

But, I realise this minute, I am a fool. A complete fool. The above news item came from a **1972** paper, not **1971**. I leave it here because next year I will probably appear a philistine again. So, let me get in first and stop that thought.

Quixotic, isn't it.

HELPING THE BAFFLED VOTER

Letters, (Mrs) M Diesner. Now that the local government elections are over and it is apparent that only a minority of people eligible to vote did so, the old argument will come up as to whether voting should be compulsory or not.

The usual reason given to explain why so few people vote is that Australians are apathetic. I suggest that the word should be baffled.

I live within 50 yards of a polling booth. I take an interest in the workings of the local council, and yet I did not vote. I passed a booth a few times but in the end squibbed it. I could not face voting for someone about whom I knew nothing. Of course, I had read the pamphlets thrust in the letterbox, containing such meaningless messages as "Bloggs for Action," "Smith for lower rates," but no worthwhile information.

Any racegoer who wants to bet an odd dollar has a form guide supplied by the newspapers. Why could it not be compulsory for the council to send a potted biography of each candidate to the voters, or, alternatively, have these biographies published in the local paper and displayed in the local library or council chambers? These biographies, which must be certified true, should include something on the aims and attitudes of the candidates.

Discussion with my non-voting friends reveals the same basic reason for failure to vote. Consequently, compulsory elections would be no more meaningful than they are now. At one compulsory election, faced with a list of unknowns, I voted for all the Irish names; at another, for all the Scots. Perhaps the best men won. Who knows?

VOTING BAFFLED.

Letters, E Stevens. Referring to local government elections, the word "baffled" suggested by Mrs M Diesner seems more appropriate than the usual "apathetic."

In my own electorate, or ward, of Lawson, one candidate who got 41 primary votes beat another who got 1,163. Who wouldn't be baffled over that one? The crazy system of preferential voting has gone too far.

HOUSEHOLDER PROBLEMS

Letters, K Starr. Now that we have a new Prime Minister, I would like to draw the attention of his department to something which my mother considers unfair to human beings.

This is the sales tax on toothpaste.

There is no sales tax on soap for dogs. Does this mean that the Federal Government considers that hair on dogs, which I suppose would be lucky to live for 15 years, is more important to the nation's health than our teeth?

Letters, B Mychael. Your correspondent Mrs Aileen Greenaway suggests that rather than introduce an optional examinable subject, Biblical studies, into our school curriculum, we introduce a course of general theology.

While agreeing that the knowledge of other people's beliefs may help towards living in peace and understanding with them, it must not be forgotten that so few of our children have any knowledge, even at a basic level, of Bible teachings. And without this background, how can they be expected to understand and appreciate other beliefs?

Letters, R B. I usually have morning coffee in one of the city cafes, for which I paid 20c until recently. Then the charge was increased to 25c. Upon my inquiry why, the reply was because of increased wages.

Our local automatic laundry just increased the prices for one washing from 40c and 80c (depending on the size of the machine) to 60c and $1.20, an increase of 50 per cent. Upon my inquiry why, the reply was the same: increased wages.

Regularly my wife buys soap, detergents and other household cleaners, for which she has paid until recently (they are always the same items) $3.44 in one of the stores which "reduced the prices of over 3,000 items." She is paying now $4.87 for same, an increase of about 40 per cent.

One can have different thoughts about labour unions and Mr Hawke's action, but to my way of thinking his is the first positive action to bridle the unrestricted and uninhibited chase for higher and higher profits.

The impotence of the now three-year-old Trade Practices Act is demonstrated in that so far, not one prosecution has taken place. One can hardly refrain from thinking that the Act was not really meant to restrain unfair trade practices.

Or is exploitation fair trading?

ADVANCE AUSTRALIA FAIR

The Australian National Anthem and Flag Quests Committee is obviously a most select body, charged with serious Matters of State. It had run a survey to ask for suggestions from the public for the purpose of creating a new flag for the nation.

It received "many hundred" proposals, though this compares badly with the 1951 figure of over 30,000. The *SMH* Editor thought the idea of a new flag was bad. "The arguments presented are feeble, or downright silly, and none can be considered to have widespread appeal."

One argument against the current flag talked about the Union Jack in its corner It goes on about how it represents the power and influence of another nation, Britain, which in this day and age, has no official role to play in Australia. And it signified a subservience that , if ever Australians felt in the past, they no longer felt today.

The Editor replied that Britain was part of our history, and many of its institutions still permeated every thing we based our current society on. To reject the Unions Jack would be to reject our history, a history that we should be proud of.

Of course, the flag was not changed. But every now and then, since 1971, some groups try to make this happen. I especially remember one attempt about 30 years ago that suggested the Boxing Kangaroo as the central motif. There was a lot of support for this mighty beast, but despite its long history in Australia, it could not get the vote of the people.

ASIAN MIGRATION INTO AUSTRALIA

Australia's White Australia Policy has by now just about bitten the dust. In its most recent form, it was based on the hatred that Australians deeply felt for the Japanese from the start of the Pacific War in 1941. It spread, almost without thinking, to other Asians and still permeated the minds of many good people here. Especially if members of their family had suffered at Japanese hands.

But by 1971, most people were happy to say that all Asians might be admitted to Australia. The official system at the time allowed for a small number of coloured persons to enter our country. But it seemed that most of the population would have readily accepted larger numbers if the politicians would face up to the risk of proposing an increase.

In NSW, the Premier was Bob Askin, a wily and skilled politician. He made a speech in which he said that "while they have equal rights with us as human beings, but when it comes to living together and trying to assimilate, it just does not work."

He went on. "I have seen some of the things happening in the United States, with their extreme racial problems, and what is happening in Britain and South Africa and many other parts of the world. We would be setting up a system for which we would pay dearly in years to come."

Other people has a few words to say on this.

Letters, P Noakes. Mr Askin's comments on coloured immigration imply a gross insult to the majority of Australians. He implies that Australians are so bigoted and prejudiced that the presence of more coloured immigrants in Australia would automatically lead to hatred and violence.

Mr Askin repeats several times that he is not a racist, which is good news. But he certainly seems to be a cynic. I, for one, do not accept his assertion that if more coloured immigrants came to this country, a "racial problem" would inevitably develop. Of course, if hundreds of thousands of migrants came into this country very rapidly, problems of unemployment and hardship would develop. But I know of no political party which proposes to "open the floodgates" to migrants. As I understand it, the Labor Party's policy involves a slowing down of all forms of migration.

In my prejudiced way, I believe that a Negro doctor or a Japanese lawyer would make a better contribution to Australia than an Italian labourer or a Yugoslav cleaner. If I might paraphrase Mr Askin's remark: "If it is properly and fairly handled, immigration will be a winner for Australia."

Letters, P Hastings. The third problem is the rate of assimilation. We should not go so far as to provoke and alarm those racist Australians to whom Mr Askin is appealing. That would be politically dangerous at home and abroad but we can still have an imaginative, generous, coloured immigration program and avoid the problems of the UK.

Using immigration problems for short-term political advantage is a nasty game. Mr Askin may have been applauded for alluding to race situations in the US and South Africa which have no parallel here, and need never have, and for his reckless allegation that certain sections of the

Labor Party advocate "....opening of the floodgates to coloured immigration" (which Labor leaders ever advocated that?), but he did his party and country a disservice. Mr Askin wasn't discussing immigration problems; he was helping to create them.

Letters, R Klugman, MP for Prospect. P Noakes justifiably attacks Mr Askin's cynical racism, but shows his own prejudices quite clearly.

He says, "I believe that a Negro doctor or a Japanese lawyer would make a better contribution to Australia than an Italian labourer or a Yugoslav cleaner."

To have prejudices as a group against the unskilled and those coming from Mediterranean rather than "Nordic" countries is no real advance on Mr Askin. To make value judgments of people, on the basis of their education or their ethnic origin, rather than as individuals, is very closely related to racism.

FAMILY LAW

The Letter below points out the number of injustices that still beset the parties to proceeding to a divorce.

Letters, M Kennett. The Act itself seems strangely grudging and illiberal, as if it regards every person involved in divorce litigation as a potential "guilty party" rather than a hapless participant in a human tragedy. But an even greater problem is presented by the practically unlimited powers the Act gives to the courts.

For consider what a divorce court judge can do. He can declare one partner or the other to be the "guilty party" and pronounce the degree of "guilt"; he can grant divorce or refuse it; he can decide who is to pay the costs (almost invariably it is the man, win or lose) and assess the amount of alimony to be paid; he can order a man out of his home, thus separating him from his children, and require him to stay away even as long as a year or more, without a single charge against him having been proved; he can take the home from one partner and give it to the other, and - most dread power of all - he can give the children to one parent or the other or take them away from their parents altogether.

Concerning these wide powers conferred on the judges two things should be noted. First, every decision thus made affects very closely the most intimate lives of the persons concerned, yet they are made by one man and one man alone, with only the assertions and denials made in a restricting law-court atmosphere for him to go on and no additional information gleaned from any external inquiries.

In such circumstances, it is unlikely that a judge will gain more than a superficial acquaintance with the facts; the ultimate causes of the tragedy will remain, like the bulk of the iceberg, below the surface, unseen.

The second is that, in a democratic structure, no group, whether of politicians, public servants, scrutiny, accompanied of course by adequate public discussion.

All these conditions are inherent in the present inadequate methods of dealing with marital breakdowns. Moves have been made in other countries to introduce more seemly and humane methods, such as family courts and non-fault divorce, and it is time our own Matrimonial Causes Act, based as it is on the social conditions, misconceptions, fears and prejudices of a less enlightened age, was drastically amended.

Comment. The problems that existed at the time of writing were addressed by the Family Law Act of 1975. Gough Whitlam, now Prime Minister, correctly perceived that this was an area of law that was crying out for reform. He changed the laws. For example, he said that divorce should be without blame. Just get on with the matter, and forget who had been the goodie and who the baddie.

He also set up a new system of Family Courts that covered all States, except Western Australia. It specialised in famlily matters such as divorce, and appointed judges for long terms. These helped straighten out the mess. The system we have now is based on that Act. It works better that the old one.

But it is not perfect. For example, critics talk about the secrecy provisions that protect the parties. But they also protect the judges from proper scrutiny. Others claim that the Court is biased towards women. Be that as it may, the end result is better than it was.

DECEMBER NEWS ITEMS

NSW and Victoria are jointly going after the failed pyramid marketing company Vardin. The pyramid way of selling is under more and more scrutiny as various proponents find themselves in financial problems...

But it is not just the giants that are in trouble. The housewives who sold cosmetics and the like, in their own small time businesses, are being left with piles of stock that they cannot sell.

IATA is a body that represents all of the major airlines that fly international routes. Qantas is a member but plans to defy it. It will drop its fare to Britain to $700 whereas the IATA agreed fare if $1,300....

Qantas wants to increase traffic on the route to Australia, but its efforts are being hampered by the fixed IATA rates. So, it has said, we will cut fares, and if that causes IATA troubles, too bad.

Bob Menzies, former Prime Minister, had a stroke in his home in Victoria. This was his second stroke, and slightly paralysed his right side. Fortunately he recovered fully, and lived until 1978.

A number of Sydney suburbs had showers of golden rain drop on them. Showers lasted a full five minutes....

Analysis found that the rain was actually the excreta from swarms of bees who dropped undigested pollen down the hatch.

The Honeymoon period for the new Prime Minister is just about over. Criticism of his performance is coming from all sides, even within his own Party....

The latest news from this front is that the DLP has attacked him, saying that he is no different from John Gorton, his predecessor. Their claim is that he is doing nothing to advance the country, and that his management of the economy is far too conservative and hackneyed....

Popular support for his attractive wife remains solid.

The well-known Australia opera singer, Marie Collier, at age 44, died when she fell from the sixth floor of her apartment in London. She was attempting to force open a window and slipped.

The cricket tour that had been planned, after the South African players were barred, is all ready to start playing Tests. The so-called World Eleven has had a practice match in Brisbane, and is now in Adelaide ready to give Australia a taste of the leather and willow....

This tour will go ahead.

With that, **I will now give my quill back to the family duck.** I have written 33 Titles in this series, and their acceptance around this fair country has been most gratifying....

So I wish you and the nation **all the best for the future.** We have a great nation, and I do hope we can keep it that way. **I urge you to act if all that starts to change.**

TOP MOVIES

Airport	Burt Lanchaster
Patton	George C Scott
Love Story	Ali MacGraw
M*A*S*H	Don' Sutherland
Tora! Tora! Tora!	Martin Balsam
Five Easy Pieces	Jack Nicholson
Ryan's Daughter	Robert Mitchum
Women in Love	Glenda Jackson
Darling Lily	Julie Andrews
I Never Sang for my Father	Gene Hackman
Lovers and other Strangers	Dianne Keaton
Cromwell	Richard Harris
The Great White Hope	Hal Holbrook

ACADEMY AWARDS

Best Male Actor	George C Scott
Best Female Actor	Glenda Jackson
Best Movie	Patton
Best Documentary	Woodstock

TOP OF THE POPS

Eagle Rock	Daddy Cool
My Sweet Lord	George Harrison
The Pushbike Song	The Mixtures
Daddy Cool	Drummond
L.A. International Airport	Susan Raye
Don't know how to love him	Helen Reddy
Knock Three Times	Dawn
Banks of the Ohio	O' Newton-John
Rose Garden	Lynn Anderson
Eleaner Rigby	Zoot
Too Young to be Married	The Hollies
Love is a Beautiful Song	Dave Mills
Maggy May	Rod Stewart
I think I love you	Partridge Family
Bond of Gold	Freda Payne
It's a Sin to Tell a Lie	Gerry Monroe
Me and Booby McGee	Janis Joplan

THE FINAL CHAPTER

In this Chapter, I will spend a fair bit of time closing out some of the ongoing stories from earlier months.

But I won't be ignoring other matters. For example, I can't ignore the joys of Christmas. And I must ponder for a while on what might happen in Australia in the future.

GUNNING GOATS

I realise when I sum up the contents of this book that I have spent most of my time talking about city affairs. And I have not paid much attention to what's happening in the country, especially in the bush.

So, as reparation for this oversight, I have included the following Letter. It is pure unadulterated bush. The Heading was taken from the *SMH,* and it means as much to me as it does to most readers.

Letters, D Mountfort. I read with great interest the article on goats, to think that at last graziers are now realising their value in monetary terms.

In 1929 I was employed as a station hand on Little Wilga Station between Coolabah and Bobby Mount in the far west of NSW. There was a bad drought on at the time and the place was overrun with wild goats, particularly in the out-station on the hills.

The manager told me that if I liked, he would provide the ammunition and I could shoot them (I had a 32-20 Savage repeater rifle in those days). Also, I could have the skins and the "fat." He would pay me sixpence a scalp for my trouble (to a boy of 21 earning 26/6 a week it seemed a good idea).

So on the Good Friday in 1929 I took out my dogs and we rounded up hundreds of the goats and used up the 200 cartridges my boss had given me. Well, here was I some 8-10 miles from the boundary-rider's hut, where I lived with "Old Bill" the boundary-rider, and with 200 goats all dead. I was satisfied with the sixpence a scalp so smartly cut the scalps off.

On the Sunday (Easter Sunday) I was enjoying the day "washing and cooking dampers and sea pies" when the boss arrived in his 1928 Dodge ute and said to me: "My, you have made havoc with the goats - how many did you shoot?" I replied, "Some 200." He then said: "Well, you will have to burn the carcasses, you know; you cannot leave them for the flies to blow otherwise we will have the place overrun with blowflies."

So on the Easter Monday I had to take the horse and dray, drive eight miles and burn the wretched things. To make matters worse I had done the shooting on a huge clay-pan over a mile in diameter.

I got home about 9pm a very tired and more experienced "Pommy" migrant.

Comment. There. That should satisfy my readers in the bush. That's more attention than they get from newspapers, authorities, and Politicians.

THE VIETNAM WAR

If this war was a hot topic at the start of the year, it was only warm at the end. Of course, parents and wives and siblings and neighbours were still frantically worried about the lives of their sons. And the worry was with them every minute of every day.

But, the number of men in uniform had been reduced a lot, and it looks like further reductions were on the card. Also, there was a small but noticeable reduction in the intensity of the war. That helped.

But beyond that, America was getting to the stage where it was fully disillusioned with the war, and their troops too were being brought home. On top of all that, President Nixon was right now preparing to go to China, amid certain fan-fare, and will start to talk to the Chinese with an agenda that surely would cover the conflict.

And, if China stopped fighting, there could be no chance that the Vietcong would continue.

To sum up, while it was true that our lads were being killed there daily, the prospects that peace would come soon were the best they had been for years.

Footnote. Nixon did visit China in 1972, and his tour was a great success. He paved the way for gradual troop removals from Vietnam, and in 1973, the final forces were rehabilitated.

LABOR VERSUS LIBERALS

The Liberal Party was doing it tough. John Gorton was a popular Prime Minister but had none of the dynamism that the population was ready for. Williams McMahon, Gorton's successor as Prime Minister, was not found to be engaging and his policies were just a continuation of the Liberal Party's agenda for the last twenty years.

Further, the performance of the Liberals in State elections had been disappointing.

Most of all, the Party was again ripping itself apart over issues such as leadership and policies. Almost daily, the papers were full of stories of how so-and-so was about to launch a bid for the top Job. Little factions came and went in the twinkling of an eye. Even if Labor offered no challenge, you would bet that McMahon could not last another year.

But Labor **did** have a challenge, personified by Gough Whitlam. The policies that he was espousing were people-based, and not ideologically-based.

He was now preaching to the hip-pockets of the nation. He weaved a story about better education, changes to the Family Court, promotions for the public servants, better hospitals and Medical Benefits schemes, and improved housing. He appealed to voters who were ready for change, and no longer wanted the staus quo.

Comment. If you had asked me now, at the end of 1971, what the result of next years' election would be, I would have said without a doubt that Whitlam and Labor were certain to win.

Footnote. Whitlam **did** indeed win the 1972 election. He increased his seats in the House by 12 , and thus sat comfortably there for two years.

CHRISTMAS CHEER

Well, it had to happen. Christmas is here. This is my 33rd book, and in each of them I have said that this is my dread time for the year. All those little children enjoying themselves and screaming and belting drums and shooting guns and wearing dresses. And the adults are all so jolly when really they are all worried about something. All the people I have to shake hands with, and pretend I like them.

As I said, for 33 Books I have talked jaundicedly about these. But this year I will be good, and not even mention them.

This year, my list of the good presents that you can give is written for the Mums. Real adult stuff, and for once the children miss out. What a great everyday selection to choose from.

Feminine fripperies at Dorith Unger's! As a result of a buying tour, she has a staggering collection of lovely wisps of sleepwear and gowns. Sketched is an enchanting gypsy-look nightie, just one of a collection with embroidered designs - others in dreamy styles and fabrics, some with lashings of lace. As well, brunch coats and gowns to give 'the belle of the ball' feeling, even in the boudoir - others for lounging around viewing TV and feeling elegant. There's a snag, though - how to choose ONE from such a scene of feminine splendours? If in doubt, give a gift voucher from Dorith Unger, 37-39 Castlereagh St. Still at the same address!

Carita's Miracle Wave! Carita's newest Protein Body Wave has been a sensational success! Even "difficult to hold" hair responds beautifully to this kindest of all lotions. Hair is left shiny, bouncy - and FULL of vitality! You want to look your very best at Xmas - and you can do it, so easily, by calling into any of the three conveniently located Carita Salons. Their International hair stylists can achieve absolute miracles with any type of hair.... and are expert at giving the finished product that extra "little something" in flattery that makes all the difference! Carita, at Woollahra; Edgecliff; and Rose Bay.

Cute Hostess Apron! Are you all set for guests? If so, you'll appreciate the Rodrequez hostess apron - snap one up for yourself, and more as gifts for your friends who like to entertain. They're in delicious fade-free colour combinations, and feature a large centre pocket - price $2.95. Another "spot-on" gift would be a 1972 Wall hanging Calendar. We like the gaiety of their fade-free colours and designs - 6 from which to choose! The size is 38in deep by 12in wide - price $2.50. These budget-price gifts are available at all gift shops - Wedgewood, Double Bay; Line Bush, Mosman; Driftwood Gifts, Newport and David Jones'.

Family Gift, $4.95. If your children are studying languages, you can't give them anything better than a course from the World Language Records series. It will give their studies a terrific boost - and the records can be of use to intending travellers in the family as well! In fact, it's a gift that will keep on giving for years - and, goodness knows, they're inexpensive enough! Only $4.95 a course for 5 LP 7in records, playing at 33 1/2 RPM, plus a book to help with easy pronunciation and English translation.... In French, Italian, Spanish, Indonesian, German and Hebrew, from David Jones', Grace Bros, Waltons and Big W.

North Shore Sheers! Whenever we drop into Heppy's at Chatswood, we find them busy, busy, busy! No wonder, they have such stocks of fashions at value-wise prices! Xmas party dresses are delectable, especially popular being sheers - long shirred sheers from $26, with lovely floral long shirtmakers, $46.50. The sheer ensemble sketched would be a gem to wear to weddings (perfect for the bride's mother!) in burnished gold, muted green or turquoise, $52. Also sketched is a jersey terrace dress, colourful in hot pink and Parma violet, $26.... other long dresses and caftans in dry-dry fabrics and cottons. As well, a host of short gay dresses for the holidays from $6, also Osti fashons at Heppy's, Chatswood.

SUMMING UP 1971

How did we fare over the year? We started with a full scale Vietnam war and ended with one that was almost on its last legs. We started with the Americans hating every Red in the world, but now talking about shaking hands with the Chinese Reds. That has to be an improvement.

a large scale, and virtually get away with it,

Mr Brown almost got away with it, but the long arm of the law caught up with him.

But the general public delighted that Mr Nobody took on a major institution, and hoodwinking half a million Dollars out of them.

The opponents of the South African tour had a victory when they got good numbers to demonstate, and this carried over to the banning of the tour, But, in the long run, Apartheid survived for years thereafter, and it is dubious whether the restraints on sport did anything material to stop its path. Except, maybe, to take away from the servile the pleasure that international sport gave them.

I have only touched tangentially on the Australian economy. But it was chugging along alright, but only just alright. It was under the shadow of the opening of the European Common Market, but it was clear that we could find new markets if we had to. So despite our politicians and interested groups rabbiting on about it, it was not a big worry.

Summing up, then, I saw 1971 as moderate, safe year, with international affairs better at its end. The population was well employed, well fed, and there were more safety blankets around the unfortunates that in any other country.

Maybe we can do better next year, but if we can't and we stay in the same place, that won't be too bad. In any case, I hope you get much enjoyment and prosperity out of it. And indeed, for many years to come.

READERS' COMMENTS

Tom Lynch, Speers Point. Some history writers make the mistake of trying to boost their authority by including graphs and charts all over the place. You on the other hand get a much better effect by saying things like "he made a pile". Or "every one worked hours longer than they should have, and felt like death warmed up at the end of the shift." I have seen other writers waste two pages of statistics painting the same picture as you did in a few words.

Barry Marr, Adelaide You know that I am being facetious when I say that I wish the war had gone on for years longer so that you would have written more books about it.

Edna College, Auburn. A few times I stopped and sobbed as you brought memories of the postman delivering letters, and the dread that ordinary people felt as he neared. How you captured those feelings yet kept your coverage from becoming maudlin or bogged down is a wonder to me.

Betty Kelly, Wagga Wagga. Every time you seem to be getting serious, you throw in a phrase or memory that lightens up the mood. In particular, in the war when you were describing the terrible carnage of Russian troops, you ended with a ten-line description of how aggrieved you felt and ended it with "apart from that, things are pretty good here". For me, it turned the unbearable into the bearable, and I went from feeling morbid and angry back to a normal human being.

Alan Davey, Brisbane. I particularly liked the light-hearted way you described the scenes at the airports as American, and British, high-flying entertainers flew in. I had always seen the crowd behaviour as disgraceful, but your light-hearted description of it made me realise it was in fact harmless and just good fun.

MORE INFORMATION ON THESE BOOKS

Over the past 17 years the author, Ron Williams, has written this series of books that present a social history of Australia in the post-war period. They cover the period for 1939 to 1973, with one book for each year. Thus there are 35 books.

To capture the material for each book, he worked his way through the Sydney Morning Herald and the Age/Argus day-by-day, and picked out the best stories, ideas and trivia. He then wrote them up into about 180 pages of a year-book.

He writes in a simple direct style, he has avoided statistics and charts, and has produced easily-read material that is entertaining, and instructive, and charming.

They are invaluable as gifts for birthdays, Christmas, and anniversaries, and for the oldies who are hard to buy for.

These books are available at all major retailers such as Dymocks and Collins. Also at on-line retailers such as Booktopia and Amazon, and your local newsagent.

Over the next few pages, summaries of other books in the Series are presented. A synopsis of all books in the Series is available from www.boombooks.biz

****

THERE ARE 35 TITLES IN THIS SERIES
From 1939 to 1973

Born in 1939?
What else happened?
Australian Social History

Ron Williams

In 1939. Hitler was the man to watch. He bullied Europe, he took over a few countries, and bamboozled the Brits. By the end of the year, most of Europe ganged up on him, and a phony war had millions of men idling in trenches eating their Christmas turkeys. Back home in Oz, the drunkometer was breathless awaited, pigeon pies were on the nose, our military canteens were sometimes wet and sometimes dry. Sinatra led his bobby-soxers, while girls of all ages swooned for crooner Bing.

In 1948, there was no shortage of rationing and regulation. The concept of free medicine was

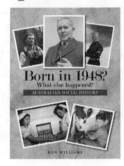

Born in 1948?
What else happened?
AUSTRALIAN SOCIAL HISTORY

RON WILLIAMS

introduced, but doctors (still controlled from Britain) would not co-operate, so that medicines on the cheap were scarcely available to the public. Burials on Saturday were banned. Rowers in Oxford were given whale steak to beat meat rationing.

****

Chrissi and birthday books for Mum and Dad and Aunt and Uncle and cousins and family and friends and work and everyone else.

Don't forget a good read and chuckle for yourself.

In 1957, Britain's Red Dean said Chinese Reds were OK. America avoided balance-of-payments problems by sending entertainers here. Sydney's Opera House will use lotteries to raise funds. The Russians launched Sputnik and a dog got a free ride. A bodkin crisis shook the nation. After the Suez crisis last year, many nations were acting tough. The Middle East was on the point of eruption..

In 1958, the Christian brothers bought a pub and raffled it. Circuses were losing animals at a great rate. Officials were in hot water because the Queen Mother wasn't given a sun shade; it didn't worry the lined-up school children, they just fainted as normal. School milk was hot news, bread home deliveries were under fire. The RSPCA was killing dogs in a gas chamber. A tribe pointed the bone at Albert Namatjira; he died soon after.

****

AVAILABLE AT ALL GOOD BOOK STORES AND NEWSAGENTS

In 1967, postcodes were introduced, and you could pay your debts with a new five-dollar note. You could talk-back on radio, about a brand new ABS show called "This Day Tonight." Getting a job was easy with unemployment at 1.8%. Arthur Calwell left at last. Whitlam took his place. Harold Holt drowned, and Menzies wrote his first book in retirement.

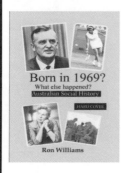

In 1969. Hollywood produced a fake movie that appeared to show a few Americans walking on the moon. The Indian Pacific crossed the nation for the first time. There are now no Labor governments in office in all Australia, but Paul Keating just got a seat in Canberra. Thousands of people walked the streets in demos against the Vietnam War, and HMAS Melbourne cut a US Destroyer in two. The Poseidon nickel boom made the fortunes of many Oz Magazine died an untimely death.

****